THE HERITAGE SERIES

SERIES TITLES

Under the Pines
Ada J. Moore | M. Wade Mahon & Lillian S. Mahon (eds.)

From Madison to Mobile: The Diary of Corporal Samuel Burdick, Jr.
Samuel Burdick, Jr. | Daniel Scharfenberg (ed.)

The Yesterdays of Grand Rapids
Charles Belknap | Colleen Alles (ed.)

The Wisconsin Idea
Charles McCarthy | Ross K. Tangedal & Jeff Snowbarger (eds.)

"When I attain to utter forth in verse
Some inward thought, my soul throbs audibly
Along my pulses, yearning to be free"
                    "The world is weak,
And what we best conceive, we fail to speak."

MRS. BROWNING

UNDER THE PINES

poems

ADA J. MOORE

edited by

M. Wade Mahon & Lillian S. Mahon

CORNERSTONE PRESS
UNIVERSITY OF WISCONSIN-STEVENS POINT

Cornerstone Press, Stevens Point, Wisconsin 54481
Copyright © 2026 M. Wade Mahon & Lillian S. Mahon
www.uwsp.edu/cornerstone

Printed in the United States of America.

Library of Congress Control Number: 2026940950
ISBN: 978-1-968148-54-6

Under the Pines was originally published in 1875 by West & Co., Milwaukee, Wisconsin. The work is in the public doman and is therefore not subject to copyright protection.

The epigraph features lines from "Insufficiency" (1844) by Elizabeth Barrett Browning: 1–3, 9, 11.

Cornerstone Press titles are produced in courses and internships offered by the Department of English at the University of Wisconsin–Stevens Point.

DIRECTOR & PUBLISHER
Dr. Ross K. Tangedal

EXECUTIVE EDITORS
Jeff Snowbarger, Freesia McKee

EDITORIAL DIRECTOR
Brett Hill

SENIOR EDITORS
Paige Biever, Lhea Owens

PRESS STAFF
Karlie Harpold, Sam Bjork, Sophie McPherson, Elizabeth Kyser, Andrew Bryant, Leo Poskozim, Asher Schroeder, John Evans

TO

MY LOVED AND VENERATED FATHER,

REV. DR. HALL,

Of Vermont,

THIS LITTLE VOLUME IS

AFFECTIONATELY DEDICATED,

In the hope that it may

BRIGHTEN WITH A NEW PLEASURE,

The Eightieth Year

Of a Life of Rare Beauty and

Usefulness.

CONTENTS

Introduction by M. Wade Mahon   xiii

Preface   1

- UNDER THE PINES -

Lucifer Watching the Progress of Creation   4
The Young Wife   8
Through the Pines   9
To My Husband   10
Shadows   12
My Autumn Flower   13
On the First Anniversary of My Marriage   15
Moonlight Thoughts   16
Among the Mountains   18
Love in Heaven   20
Go in Peace   21
Musings   22
My Graves   23
In the Depths   25
Alone   26
Under the Stars   27
Lines for the Times   28
Baby Florence   30
"As Good As Ever Were Caught"   31
Reaching Upward   32
Memories   33
Little Carl   34
Far Away   35
Buried Seed   36
My Lost Jewels   38
September   40

A Wish Unwished 41
Mount Mansfield 43
Moonlight on the Snow 45
Little Maud 46
A Memory 47
An Invocation 48
Under the Oaks 49
Nature's Ministry 50
April 52
Strength in Suffering 53
August 55
The Wife's Vigil 56
To "La Petite" 57
May Flowers 58
Nellie 59
Wherefore 60
"Why Wakest Thou?" 61
December 62
Hattie May 63
The Snow Blockade 64
Lines Suggested by "Buried Loves" 65
A Plea for Matrimony 66
After the Rain 69
Love's Escapade 70
On the Occasion of a Silver Wedding 72
The Wife's Greeting 73
Aspirations 74
Despondency 75
Naming the Baby 76
In Memoriam 77
A Welcome 78
The Convalescent 79
Blue Gentians 80
Once More 81
George Reed 83

- SONGS OF THE WAR -

What Shall the End Be?	87
God In History	89
To Lieutenant Maury	90
The Wounded Soldier Gathering Violets	92
The Defeat of Our Armies	93
The Fourth of July, 1863	94
Seed-Time and Harvest	95
Thoughts at a Pic-Nic	97
A Rallying Song	98
Wisconsin to Missouri	99
White and Black	101

- EARLY POEMS -

Summer Days	104
The Cry of the Heathen	105
Death of Rev. James Gallagher	106
Twilight Fancies	108
The Contrast	109
On the Death of a Babe	110
Introspection	111
To My Father on His Sixtieth Birthday	113
Midnight Musings	114
The Angel's Mission	115
Cora: A Temperence Sketch	116

Appendix: Miscellaneous Newspaper Items	121
Acknowledgments	133

Introduction

M. Wade Mahon

Heaven is free from shadows,
All is perfect, pure ethereal light;
In the Holy City shall every ransomed spirit
Wear its blood-bought robe of spotless white.

—"Shadows"

Ellen E. Phillips died August 24, 1877, after a long illness. Her gravestone in Stevens Point's Forest Cemetery includes the above lines from the final stanza of a poem published in *Under the Pines,* a collection of her work that Cornerstone Press is reissuing a little more than 150 years after it first appeared in 1875. The sentiment of faith in a better world after death is one prominent theme found in the poems she wrote over more than twenty years in her "pine cottage" near the Wisconsin River. Many of these feature the persona of a woman gazing out at the night sky after her family has gone to bed and meditating on the joys and sorrows of this life and the mysteries of the life to come.

Above these lines on her gravestone is the title to a different poem, "My Lost Jewels," one of several poems in which she mourns the three children, her "jewels," she had lost in short succession between 1858 and 1860. In "My Graves," she writes:

Upon the cold, cold snow I kneel,
  Beside my little graves,
My heart so cold I scarcely feel
  The wind that round me raves.
Here, side by side, my darlings rest,
  Amidst the wintry storm,

> Who lately to a mother's breast
>   Were folded close and warm.

In 1864 she returns to this spot, where a marble obelisk now marks their graves, to meditate on her daughter Florence and son Carl playing nearby, "with the burial grove in sight,/ Where three little forms of clay/ Slumber through a dreamless night" ("A Wish Unwished"). Both Carl (d. 1894) and Florence (d. 1918) outlived their mother and are buried a few feet away from their siblings and their parents. In all, she gave birth to at least eight children, only three of whom survived childhood.

These gravestones and the sentiments inscribed upon them, as well as the poems she wrote reflect Victorian ideas about children, marriage, faith, and death. Consistent with the times in which she lived, Phillips's poems often display an impatience with the "shadows" of this world and a longing for the "perfect, pure ethereal light" of heaven. In a world in which hardships like the loss of children to disease were less common, such positivity might come across as little more than superficial sentimentality. However, her honest appraisal of the details of her life, whether tragic, mundane, or joyful, lends depth and poignance to the works in this collection. They also tell a story of polished New England literary culture being transplanted into the newly settled "western" hinterlands of Wisconsin.

Ellen E. Phillips (1832–1877)

Ellen Phillips was born Ellen Eliza Hall in 1832 in Andover, Massachusetts, where her father, the Rev. Samuel Read Hall was head of the English Academy at the famed Phillips Academy (no relation to her future husband). Before her fifth birthday, Ellen lost her mother, after having lost three of her siblings around the same time. Her father, to whom she dedicated *Under the Pines*, became her primary mentor, both in her religious thought and educational achievements. Prior to his appointment at the Phillips Andover Academy, Samuel Read Hall had opened the country's first teacher training school, or "normal school," in Concord, Vermont and was influential in educational reform efforts throughout New England. Other educational "firsts" attributed to him include being the "pioneer of the use of the blackboard as a school room appliance."[1]

Not long after the death of Ellen's mother, the Hall family moved back to Vermont where her father served as a Congregationalist minister and

---

[1] Mahala Nyberg, "Recognizing Educator and Innovator Samuel Read Hall," *The North Star Monthly*, September 24, 2024.

educator. At Craftsbury Academy, her father's school, Ellen distinguished herself academically and "was almost precocious, early showing rare talent in the acquirement of languages and in the composition both of prose and poetry. Many of the former students of Craftsbury academy remember with pleasure the slight figure, the prominent forehead, the twinkling black eyes, and the ready wit of Ellen Hall."[2]

In 1851, she began publishing poems and short stories under the pen names of "Ada Moore," then "Jessie Moore," and later consolidated as "Ada J. Moore." Her first published work, "Early Days," which appeared in the *Orleans County Gazette*, describes the transition from carefree days of childhood—"Days of pleasure, days of spring"—to the uncertainties of adulthood in this "World of woe." She entered the adult world as "preceptress" at the Orleans County Grammar School, having benefitted from her father's direct instruction as well as his example as a teacher. In the spring of 1854, her responsibilities included teaching the "Common English branches" and the "Higher English, or the Languages," in addition to drawing and painting. The principal of this school was Alexander Lucius Twilight (1795–1857), the first African American to earn a degree from an American college or university (Middlebury College) and a long-time Vermont educator. He recommended her to the young women who would be boarding with her as "a person of amiable disposition and lady-like deportment" who "takes a deep interest in the moral and intellectual improvement of those placed under her care."[3]

In October 1854, Ellen married fellow Vermont native John Phillips (1823–1903), with her father officiating. John had also started out as a schoolteacher, first in Vermont, then in Illinois and Wisconsin at the same time he was studying medicine, which included courses at Rush Medical College in Chicago. In 1848 he had been one of the earliest settlers in the town of Stevens Point, where he began practicing medicine and purchasing land, both of which pursuits he continued until his death in 1903. Shortly after their wedding, the couple, along with John's elderly parents moved to Wisconsin where they lived in a home on a small hill near the Wisconsin River, a short walk from downtown Stevens Point. John Phillips operated his medical practice from this residence for half a century. Ellen identified her address as "Cottage Grove," referring to a grove of pine trees on the property, hence the title of her book "Under the Pines." Ellen gave up teaching in favor of raising a family, which became the focus of much of her poetry.

---

[2] *Express and Standard*, 2 October 1877.

[3] *Orleans County Gazette*, 4 March 1854.

Stevens Point, population 700 in 1854, was not the ideal location from which to launch a career as a poet—Ellen consistently referred to Wisconsin as "the Far West." Nor was it an easy place to begin a medical practice—despite the boast of having "the healthiest people in the world."[4] One biographer of John Phillips noted that "[f]ew realize now the amount of disagreeable labor that was entailed upon the pioneer physician. He was forced to visit patients up and down the river some forty miles."[5] But the Phillipses thrived in their frontier environment, despite its challenges.

From Newspapers to *Under the Pines*

When it first appeared in 1875, *Under the Pines* was "the only book of poems ever published in the northern part of Wisconsin" according to the *Stevens Point Journal.*[6] Far from being an obscure vanity project, it was published by a Milwaukee publisher and showcased a poet whose work was already familiar to readers throughout the state under her pen name. In fact, nearly all 83 poems had been previously published in newspapers, and mostly in Wisconsin.

Newspapers were a major publication venue for nineteenth-century poets. The works of Henry Wadsworth Longfellow, John Greenleaf Whittier, Oliver Wendell Holmes, William Cullen Bryant, Elizabeth Barrett Browning, Edgar Allen Poe, and other three-named bards regularly appeared in local newspapers across the country as well as magazines like the *Atlantic Monthly*. In addition to these big names, newspaper editors would also publish lesser known and local poets like "Ada J. Moore." Newspapers, in this way, "democratized" poetry, making literature available to a wider cross-section of society. They brought poetry out of small elite coteries and into the public sphere, allowing people from all backgrounds, and parts of the country, to contribute to and participate in literary culture.

Before she married John Phillips, Ellen had already published several poems in the *Orleans County Gazette* and other Vermont newspapers. Within months of arriving in Stevens Point she began submitting her work to the *Wisconsin Pinery,* which published at least twenty of her poems in 1855 alone. In the 1860s her works moved from the *Pinery* to the short-lived *Wisconsin States Rights* paper and then the *Wisconsin Lumberman*. In the 1860s, she also published several poems and short stories in Madison's *Wisconsin*

---

[4] *Milwaukee Daily Sentinel*, 25 January 1854.

[5] Nelke, D. I., ed. *The Columbian Biographical Dictionary and Portrait Gallery of the Representative Men of the United States,* Wisconsin Volume, Part 1. Chicago: The Lewis Publishing Company, 1895. p. 267.

[6] *Stevens Point Journal,* 9 December 1876.

State Journal, especially when the state legislature was in session, since John Phillips served in the State Assembly during these years. But her primary publishing venue was the *Milwaukee Daily Sentinel*. Between 1861 and 1873, she published more than sixty poems in this paper. She could not compete with John Greenleaf Whittier, but during her nearly 20-year writing career, her work was a regular feature in Wisconsin newspapers.

The *Stevens Point Journal* reviewer praised *Under the Pines* as having "merits far beyond and above any local interest that its publication may have excited. It contains gems in poetry that must give the writer a fame as great as her fondest ambition ever dared to hope for."[7] The collection received similar praise from reviewers in Milwaukee and Madison. The *Milwaukee Sentinel* reviewer recognized her "exquisitely poetic temperament, and it is not extravagant to say that she writes because she cannot help it. . . . [H]er power of expression equals the beauty of her conceptions, and she shows a complete and accurate mastery over a varied and effective rhythm."[8] One review, titled "A Poetess Reviews a Poetess" was written by the Madison poet Ella Wheeler (Wilcox) early in her career before she had gained a national reputation [see Appendix]. Wheeler concluded her comments with an interesting tribute to her home state:

> "Under the Pines," will repay perusal, and is a credit to its author and to Wisconsin—the state which contributes more to Eastern literature than all other Western states combined.

Another review came from a newspaper in the poet's home state of Vermont:

> The book is made up of upwards of eighty short poems on as many different subjects, some drawn from nature, some from her early associations among the green hills of our own state; some are suggested by her new western home, and some by passing events. They are all full of the poetic element, and as pure as the falling snow-flakes. We know of no book more elevating in its tone, nor one with which those little snatches of time that every one has could be more profitably spent.[9]

The Poems

In addition to personal reflections on her family, especially the precariousness of her children's lives, Phillips addresses a variety of subjects. Many

---

[7] *Stevens Point Journal,* 2 January 1875.

[8] *Milwaukee Daily Sentinel,* 24 December 1874.

[9] *Express and Standard* [Newport, VT], 16 January 1877.

reflect her strict moral principles, including her support of the Temperence movement ("Cora: A Temperence Sketch"). Her earliest work often reflects what she had been studying or teaching in school—these are more likely to contain literary allusions to British and classical literature. The undated poem "Introspection," for example, is a blank verse philosophical meditation that alludes to Sappho, Sidney's *Astrophil and Stella*, and Edward Young's "Night Thoughts." The opening poem of the book—"Lucifer Watching the Progress of Creation"—is a fascinating poem, also in blank verse, that combines imagery from Milton's *Paradise Lost* with contemporary examples of paleontology, suggesting some sort of synthesis of Darwinian evolution and the biblical creation account. This piece was published in the *Sentinel* in 1873 (one of the last ones she published); however, it seems likely that it was one she had at least started when she was younger.

Some poems include allusions to and quotations from contemporary poets—well-known figures like Elizabeth Barrett Browning, Longfellow, Tennyson, as well as lesser-known ones (to us) like Lydia Huntley Sigourney (1791–1865), to whom she wrote a "Sonnet to Mrs. Sigourney." Sigourney was best known for her "obituary poems," a very popular genre with which Phillips was well acquainted.

In 1860 John Phillips was elected to the state Assembly as a member of the recently formed Republican party. Ellen, who sometimes joined him in Madison when the Assembly was in session, continued writing personal meditations on family, faith, and the changing of the seasons. But, as her husband's public activities grew, "Ada J. Moore" expanded her public voice as well. She devotes a whole section of *Under the Pines* to "Songs of the War," which focus on the Civil War from the perspective of someone far from the front lines but who closely followed newspaper reports and observed life on the home front. These poems include meditations on the hardships of war ("God in History," "The Wounded Soldier Gathering Violets," and "White and Black") as well as criticisms of Northerners who had become "traitors" to support the Confederacy ("What Shall the End Be?" and "To Lieutenant Maury"). The first of these describes the choices of a childhood friend of hers from Vermont who had married a Southerner. Most of the poems in this section are responding to Union victories or losses during the war, including the abolition of slavery in Missouri in "Wisconsin to Missouri." Like many New Englanders, Ellen and John had brought their anti-slavery convictions with them to Wisconsin. Ella Wheeler observes:

> [t]he patriot, also, breathes in some of the poems—written during the war—and the whole volume bespeaks for the author a love of the right,

and true, and a desire to lift the burden of the oppressed, and help the suffering ones of earth, rather than an ambition for literary distinction.

The Civil War poems live up to her unionist and anti-slavery convictions, and the centrality of her Christian faith pervades her meditations on suffering, death, marriage, and nature.

In addition to war poems, she wrote about her travels, reflecting on visits to Vermont in "Among the Mountains" (1864), "Mount Mansfield" (1867), and "Once More" (1872). She occasionally weighed in on legislative debates ("The Voice of the Waters," 1864), translated French poetry ("Alone," 1865) and wrote sentimental moral fables ("The Swiss Shepherdess," 1864). She continued to write about politics and current events after the war. The poem, "Buried Seed," for instance, seems at first glance to be a simple fable about an alpine farmer; however, it turns out to be an allegory celebrating the Wisconsin Supreme Court decision in 1866 that confirmed the voting rights of Black men in Wisconsin. After the war, she also tried her hand at songwriting. Two of these songs were published, "Tell Me, Ye Falling Leaves" (1867), and "As Good as Ever Were Caught" (1868), with music composed by her collaborator *Milwaukee Sentinel* journalist, Everett Chamberlin (1839–1875). Only the latter of these was included in *Under the Pines*.

Final Years

The war years saw a brief hiatus in the growth of the Phillips family. In 1867, however, they lost another daughter, Nellie, at five months. Hattie May Phillips was born in 1869 and outlived all her siblings, living until 1962. It is likely that at least one other child died very young or in childbirth during these years—accounts differ as to how many children she had in total. The last child we know of was Pearl Estelle Phillips, who died in July 1874 at two months. It was around this time that Ellen likely compiled the poems for *Under the Pines*. Her lament for the death of Pearl, "In Memoriam," which came out in August 1874, was the last poem she published prior to the publication of the book. It is possible she was already experiencing symptoms of the illness that would take her life three years later at the young age of 44.

When she died in August 1877, only two months after the death of her father, her many friends in Wisconsin and Vermont paid tribute to her life. Childhood friends remembered Ellen fondly: "Of an ardent, impulsive temperament, and remarkably strong in her affections, she was dearly loved by all who knew her."[10] Her Wisconsin friends expressed similar sentiments.

---

[10] *Express and Standard*, 2 October 1877.

Albert G. Ellis eulogized her as having a "mind cultivated in no ordinary degree—not rudiments alone, but the more solid attainments of physics and philosophy adorned and strengthened her understanding." He remarks how she did not engage in "pedantry" in normal conversation but that "it was only her more intimate friends and family that knew of her attainments of the exact sciences and the languages."[11]

In the last years of her life, Ellen Phillips continued to write and to volunteer in various local and state organizations. In his eulogy, Albert G. Ellis observed that "To indite her works of charity, her labors of love, would only be to give a history of most of the benevolent enterprises among our lady friends, that have been had in our city over the last 23 years." Among these efforts he highlights her role in establishing a local Library Association. The first volume of this association's newsletter in Nov. 1877 included a poem by Gilbert L. Park in her honor.

These tributes from her friends and associates and the willingness of Milwaukee's West & Co. publishers to produce such a high-quality volume of her works argue that she truly deserved the title of Stevens Point's first poet laureate, if such a title had existed. Ellen Phillips' poetry is a treasure, once hidden in the dense pine grove of her frontier Victorian town, now proudly displayed in this new edition for the appreciation of a new generation of readers. *Under the Pines*, to paraphrase Longfellow, invites readers to

> Read from some humbler poet,
>   Whose songs gushed from *her* heart,
> As showers from the clouds of summer,
>   Or tears from the eyelids start;
>
> Who, through long days of labor,
>   And nights devoid of ease
> Still heard in *her* soul the music
>   Of wonderful melodies.[12]

---

[11] *Stevens Point Journal,* 1 September 1877.

[12] Longfellow, Henry Wadsworth. "Proem [The Day is Done]." *The Waif: A Collection of Poems.* Boston, 1846, x–xi.

Preface

I offer these poems—without apology for their many imperfections, not to an exacting public, but to the friends by whose desire I have been induced to publish them, who know under what circumstances they were written, and how many hours of pain and weariness they have helped to render more endurable.

THE AUTHOR.

UNDER THE PINES

"In the beginning," while, as yet, the earth
Revolved in darkness, a chaotic mass,
Lit only by its own dull smouldering fires,
That still at intervals the surface broke,—
Amidst the murky vapors that arose
From the yet seething waters, moved a Spirit
Fearful in aspect. His majestic form
Bespoke some high archangel, sent from Heaven
On glorious embassy; but in eye,
Dark with malignity and baffled rage,
And on his haughty lip, that ever curled
With fiendish sneers, and on his sin-scathed brow,
His name was branded—fallen Lucifer!
Here, as within a half-extinguished hell,
Dwelt he with all his legions. Fit abode
For spirits fallen—lifeless, stagnant gloom,
Save when the earth with fierce convulsions rocked,
Or stifling, sulphurous flames burst forth anew.
But as the dismal centuries rolled by,
With vague surprise the imprisoned spirits marked
A gradual change. A faint and shadowy light
Displaced the sullen gloom; the earthquakes raged
At longer intervals, with lessened throes;
And the fierce cauldrons of the boiling deep
At times subsided to reluctant calm;
Ere long the sloping hillsides, brown and bare,
Were faintly tinged with soft and delicate green,
Seen dimly in the twilight.

       Then appeared
On earth a mystery, and *Life* began—
Life in its lowest forms; the crawling worm,
The tiny insect, born but for a day.
With sneering wonder Lucifer beheld
This new strange creation, in *his* view
Worthless and aimless; and his demons vied
With him in blasphemy and fierce derision.
But still th' eternal years of God rolled on,
And new creative wonders had their birth.

The light grew clearer; the receding clouds
Let in brief glimpses of the blue beyond,
Wondrously beautiful, while on the earth
The verdure deepened; plants and shrubs appeared,
And soon majestic forests proudly tossed
Aloft their branches, whose soft foliage wooed
The zephyrs, newly born.

       There came a time
When Lucifer stood wrapped in gloomy thought,
And upward raised by chance his sullen gaze—
Then stood aghast. The canopy of cloud
Was rent asunder, and through countless rifts
The moon and stars looked down upon the earth.
Fixed to the spot he stood, and gnashed his teeth
In speechless agony. Too well he knew
The glorious worlds thro' which he once had roamed,
Sinless and blest; and to behold them *now*
Seemed more than even Lucifer could bear.
Ere long the scattered cloudlets sank away,
The stars grew dim, and o'er the vaulted sky
A delicate flush stole upward from the East,
And deepened into crimson. Wonderingly
The fallen spirits gathered round their chief
In vague expectancy. There was a hush;
Then came a mighty voice, "Let there be light!"
And there *was* light. Upon their startled view
Uprose the broad, bright sun!

       For a brief space
Aghast they stood, and each on other turned
His bloodshot eye. Then, with a shriek of pain
At their own hideousness, they shrank away
From the clear light, and hid themselves in caves.
But the keen mind of Lucifer, alone,
In these mysterious changes dimly saw
Some glorious and unfathomable plan
Of his great Conqueror, and pondered long
With all his powers, but pondered still in vain,
To solve its mystery. No mortal pen
May paint the anguish of that haughty soul,

Bitterly conscious that the hand of God
Was still upon him, that from his control
Escape was hopeless; yet on fire with hate,
And thirsting impotently for revenge.

   Time held its course, and still creation's plan
Deepened in mystery. Through the ocean waves,
In glittering shoals, moved higher forms of life;
Huge Ganoids,[1] fiercely armed with spine and sting,
Rhizodi,[2] trenchant-toothed, cetaceans vast,
Roamed through the sea, and each on other preyed,
With dire malignity. Their life, extinct,
Was soon renewed in higher, nobler forms,
Betokening progress of development.
Meantime, on earth, amid the densest shade
Of vast primeval forests, spring to life
The Winged tribe—Dinorni,[3] huge and grim,
And flying dragons, scaled in brilliant hues.
While on the sloping hillsides and amid
The grassy plains, appeared the animal race—
The Mastodon, immense, with glistening tusks,
The Dinotherium,[4] and the Mammoth huge.
Earth's solitudes no more were mute; the roar
Of ravenous tigers answered to the shriek
Of cave-hyenas, seeking for their prey.

   As yet, within the breast of Lucifer
The new creation's aspect had not touched
A jarring chord. There was no peace on earth;
Its molten center, like his sin-wrecked heart,
Still heaved with passionate throes; its rocky crust
Was rent by wild convulsions; from beneath,
Mountains and cliffs uprose in giant strength.
The sea invaded continents, and then
Shrank back as if in fear. O'er smiling plains

---

[1] Fish with "scales consisting of bone and an outer shiny layer resembling enamel" (Merriam Webster Dictionary). The first instance of this word was in 1839.

[2] Large prehistoric sharp-toothed freshwater fish, first identified by Sir Richard Owen in 1843.

[3] Extinct species of giant bird in New Zealand related to the moa, first identified by Sir Richard Owen in 1843.

[4] Prehistoric elephant-like creature, first identified by Johann Kaup in 1829.

And wood-crowned hills the mighty glacier swept
Its huge ice-torrents, leaving in their track
Wide desolation. But there came an age
Of peace and quiet. All the seas grew calm,
The earthquakes slumbered. In that tranquil time
Awoke the beauteous sisterhood of flowers—
Earth's fairest boon; and flocks of bright-hued birds
Came flitting on their airy wings, and filled
The groves with floods of melody, that seemed
To Lucifer's ear an echo of the songs
Once heard in Heaven. He shrieked aloud in pain,
Startling the songsters from their leafy haunts
To sudden flight. A gentler animal race
Now grazed the verdure: patient, meek-eyed kine,
The noble horse, the sportive lamb and goat,
And through the forests roamed the playful fawn
And timid hare.

            The hand of Nature paused,
And Earth, perfected, waited for her lord,—

Nor waited long. In Eden's fairest bower,
Lucifer's envious eye at length beheld
The full perfection of Jehovah's plan—
(Or so he deemed it), Adam, prince of men,
And peerless Eve, in all her queenly grace.
Here must I pause, in reverential awe,[5]
Nor dare to tread where Milton once has trod,
Portraying what befell in Paradise.

Milwaukee Daily Sentinel, 15 June 1873

---

[5] This line in the *Milwaukee Daily Sentinel* is "Here let me check my too-aspiring pen."

THE YOUNG WIFE.

A spell is on my soul to-night,
  In this strange land afar,
Flooding my brain with warmth and light,
  And all sweet thoughts that are,
As if within its chambers might
  Have burst a falling star.

I dream, but not as I was wont,
  In dreaming days of yore,
Seeking, from Fancy's giddy mount,
  To scan the future o'er.
My rapture gusheth from a fount
  Of joy unknown before.

My life is all a blissful dream
  Of happiness and love;
Bright spirits, strewing flowerets, seem
  Along my path to move,
With soft eyes, lustrous as the gleam
  Of moonlit skies above.

But there are hours—*thou* canst not guess,
  Thou of the lonely heart—
That to this life of happiness a deeper thrill impart,
  A wild, unutterable bliss,
That mocks the poet's art.

I cannot think it will abide—
  This deep and passionate bliss;
The heavenward path were never tried,
  If life were all like this;
But oh! may Passion's waves subside
  In the calm lake of Peace.

Milwaukee Daily Sentinel, 23 April 1861

THROUGH THE PINES.

Coming through the stately pines,
  When the day was growing dim,
And the songsters of the forest
  Chanted low their evening hymn,—
Tenderly my hand was taken,
  Words were murmured in my ear—
      Old words,
      Bold words,
  Timid maidens shrink to hear.

Pulling moss and plucking flowers,
  Feigned I not to understand;
From life's dearest, holiest blessing
  Coyly keeping back my hand,
As, with free and careless footsteps,
  Tripped I lightly at his side—
      Doubting,
      Pouting,
  Thinking thoughts of maiden pride.

Faster fell the shades of night,
  Darker grew the woodland path;
And the blackened trunks around us
  Rose like spectres full of wrath.
Every weird and sudden whisper
  Of the night wind made me start—
      Humbly,
      Dumbly,
  Drew I nearer to his heart.

Gently stole his arm around me,
  On my lips I felt a kiss;
Darkness fled and terror vanished
  At that thrilling touch of bliss.
Homeward through the night we went,
  With the light of love around us—
      Nearer,
      Dearer,
Grows the chain that night that bound us.

Milwaukee Daily Sentinel, 2 September 1865

Knowest thou what I would yield for thee,—
      For thee resign?
Th' uncounted wealth that paves the sea,
      Where rubies shine;
The friends, the haunts of childish glee,
      That once were mine.
For thee—without a tear—my heart
All early dreams of Fame and Art,
All hopes and loves, should bid depart,
      Save Heaven's and thine.

Know'st thou what I would *bear* for thee,—
      For thee endure?
The darkest cup of calumny
      In earth's vile sewer,
So that thine own name might be
      Stainless and pure.
All pain and agony and woe
How gladly this frail form should know
Might but thine own life-currents flow
      Healthful and sure.

Knowest thou what I would *do* for thee,—
      For thee would dare?
To the fierce bolt that rends the tree
      My breast I'd bare,
From the Death Angel's dark decree
      Thy life to spare.
Not the steep mountain's frowning height,
Not the dread Simoon's[6] withering blight,
Should stay me, in my steadfast flight
      Thy lot to share.

Knowest thou the rich, the sole reward,
      Should fain be mine?
Not all the wealth of Indias, poured
      Beneath my shrine,—

------

[6] A *simoom* is a hot, dry wind in the Arabian desert.

My love would spurn the golden hoard,
    And droop and pine.
I seek a richer, dearer boon,
The purest bliss that earth hath known—
To feel thy heart is all my own,
    That I am thine.

Pine Cottage, 1 January 1855
Wisconsin Pinery, 15 January 1855

SHADOWS.

The world is full of shadows,
  Everywhere they lie beneath the trees;
Silently and swiftly they glide along the meadows,
  Or slumber on the lake in dreamful ease.
      Where the mountain towereth,
      Where the tempest lowereth,
        Shadows ever dwell.

The heart is full of shadows,
  Those who love are ever those who fear;
Tremblingly, tho' gladly, the bride stands at the altar,
  The mother greets her first-born with a tear.
      Where our love is truest,
      Where our bliss is newest,
        Shadows ever dwell.

The soul is full of shadows,
  Sin upspringeth ever in our path;
Gloomier and darker is the shade it casteth,
  Than the storm-cloud with its gathered wrath.
      Where the wanderer strayeth,
      Where the Christian prayeth,
        Shadows ever dwell.

Heaven is free from shadows,[7]
  All is perfect, pure ethereal light;
In the Holy City shall every ransomed spirit
  Wear its blood-bought robe of spotless white.
      Where no falsehood staineth,
      Where the Savior reigneth,
        Shadows shall not dwell.

---

[7] This last stanza was quoted in the *Stevens Point Journal* obituary (1 September 1877), and the first four lines of the stanza were engraved on her gravestone, Forest Cemetery, Stevens Point, Wisconsin.

MY AUTUMN FLOWER.

Hast thou come, O gloomy Autumn!
  With thy dark and sullen brow,
And thy stormy blasts, awaking
Wild-wood wailings,—rudely shaking
  Withered foliage from the bough?

Thou hast robbed the earth of beauty!
  At thy cold and frosty breath,
All the lovely race of flowers
That have cheered the summer hours,
  Meekly bowed their heads in death.

Hushed the notes of woodland songsters,
  Warbling anthems sweet and clear,
And the wild bees' drowsy humming
'Midst the flow'rets; at thy coming
  All is mute, and sad, and drear.

Yet, within my humble cottage,
  There is joy thou canst not chill.
Here, beneath the pine tree's shade,
By thy wailing breezes swayed,
  Blooms a lovely flow'ret still.

'T is a fair and fragile blossom,
  With its blue and starry eyes,
Bathed in pearly tears of dew,
Or with wonder ever new,
  Gazing upward to the skies.

And a gentle murmur, sweeter
  Than the humming of the bee
Shrined within the rose's bosom,
While I bend o'er this sweet blossom,
  Thrills my heart with ecstasy.

Dearer far than all the flowerets
  In the Summer's crown of glee;
Lovelier, in its fragile grace,

In its winsome helplessness,
  Is this autumn flower to me.[8]

Oh! may He who gave the treasure,
  Aid us so to love and prize,
That, whene'er the Reaper come,
He may bear it hence to bloom
  In the bowers of Paradise.

Pine Cottage, 22 October 1855
Wisconsin Pinery, 25 October 1855

---

[8] Their first child, John Henry Phillips, was born 28 September 1855.

ON THE FIRST ANNIVERSARY OF MY MARRIAGE.

One happy year, dear husband,
  On rapid wing hath flown,
Since first the holy vows were breathed
  Which made our hearts as one.

I marvel not that swiftly
  Have flown the blissful hours—
"The foot of Time falls noiselessly,
  When treading only flowers."[9]

The deep, unuttered rapture
  With which that hour was rife,
When closely folded to thy breast,
  Thy lips first called me *wife*—

The constant love and kindness,
  That o'er my path have shed
A radiance that no cloud has dimmed,
  Through all the bright hours fled—

For these I bless thee, dearest,
  For all that thou hast been
To one whose life, without thy love,
  Were but a wintry scene.

And now a new emotion
  Has thrilled my heart with bliss,
Since on our babe's sweet lips I've pressed
  A mother's yearning kiss.

But all too strong the feelings
  That overwhelm my soul,
And throbbing pulses bid me seek
  Their gushings to control.

[4 October 1855]

---

[9] Variation on a couplet by English poet William Robert Spencer (1769-1834)—"How noiseless falls the foot of Time / That only treads on flowers!"—in the poem "Too Late I Stayed" (1811).

It is a calm and glorious night;
  The full moon sheds a flood of light
  Upon the soft new-fallen snow,
  Making it all one molten glow
Of wondrous radiance, wakening in my soul
A rush of thoughts too powerful for control;
Deep memories of the past—of many a night
As calmly beautiful, beneath whose light
  I've wandered with the friends of yore—
    The lovely and the brave—
  Whom I perchance shall meet no more,
  Till this mysterious life be o'er,
    And earth is in its grave.
  Fate! how widely hast thou parted
    Hearts that beat so closely then,—
  Some, to wander broken-hearted
    Through a life of care and pain,
  Some to taste earth's purest bliss,
    In domestic happiness,
    Like a weary bird, to rest,
    In the sweet, love-hallowed nest;
Others, to take a firm and noble stand
For Truth, and Freedom, and their native land,
And some, alas! to find an early grave
Beneath the green sod, or the restless wave.
  And yet—how strange—the same soft light
  That shrouds my cottage home to-night,
  O'er all these absent ones is shed,
  And on the tomb-stones of the dead,
  And many an eye, whose glance to meet,
  Would thrill me with emotions sweet,
  Is now, like mine, in ecstasy
  Upraised, thou glorious orb, to thee.
      But the voice of infancy,
    As my babe from slumber waketh,
      Steals upon my reverie,
      And the spell of memory,
    At that pleading murmur, breaketh.
And while his soft arms twine about my neck,

And I can feel his breath upon my cheek,
Or when his dark eyes, free from sin and guile,
Are raised to thrill me with his father's smile,—
The dim past fades with all its memories,
    And to my heart my child is closely pressed,
While grateful tears of joy o'erflow my eyes,
    For all the love with which my lot is blessed.

11 December 1856
Wisconsin Pinery, 18 December 1856

Among the mountains, whose rocks and fountains
    I knew, and loved in youth,
       I stand once more,
        And sadly scan them o'er,—
    Wondering if these, in truth,
Are the same scenes whose grandeur did awaken
The free proud thoughts by which my soul was shaken,
       As by a tempest, in those days of yore.

     Unchanged the mountains lift
     Their steep sides, chasm-rift,
And wood-crowned heads, to the eternal skies,
And at their feet the same calm landscape ties.
Old Owl's Head wears the frown of former time,
  Lake 'Magog smiles back with her wonted scorn,
Mansfield and Willoughby stand peerless and sublime,[10]
  As first I saw them in my childhood's morn.
     The change is in my soul,
       Since youth and I have parted;
     Who draweth near Life's midway goal,
       Must needs grow calmer hearted.

    The dew has vanished from the flowers,
    And sadder, sterner thoughts are ours.
    Yet with a tranquil and a deep delight,
     I feel myself once more among the hills;
    Lifting my eyes to yonder mountain height,
     A silent rapture all my spirit thrills,
    Better, perchance, befitting this calm spot—
    Where all, save God and Nature, is forgot,
       Than youth's impassioned gladness,
       Or wild poetic madness.

Fair scenes, adieu! To my far Western home,
  With its rich prairies and its countless flowers,
  Affection calls me; yet in future hours,

---

[10] References to peaks in northern Vermont and Lake Memphremagog on the border of Vermont and Quebec.

Memories of your sublimity shall come,
And when I sit at eve, beneath my vines,
Shall mingle with the music of the pines,
Blending the East and West in sweet harmonious chimes.

Brownington, Vermont, 20 June 1864
Wisconsin State Journal, 22 July 1864
Wisconsin Lumberman, 17 August 1864

LOVE IN HEAVEN.

"And she found new joys in her second birth,
But none like the heaven she lost on earth."[11]

HARRY VAIL.

Oh! say not, gifted bard, that Love
Finds no congenial home above,
When, freed from earthly dross and stain,
She seeks her native clime again.
Perchance indeed, she may not know
As wild a bliss as here below—
The cheek's hot flush, the gleaming eye,
The passionate idolatry,—
These are of earth, unmeet for Heaven;
Yet oh! the blessed freedom given
From doubt and jealousy and fear,
And all the woes she suffers here,—
The perfect trust, the tranquil rest,
Must make her heavenly home more blest.
Welcome the hour when Love ascends
Where soul with soul in rapture blends;
Where spirits see as they are seen,
Without a veil of earth between;
Where duty never hides regret,
Or loving hearts are "strangers yet";[12]
Where all is pure, and all is peace,
And angel raptures never cease;
Where the tear of sorrow ne'er may fall,
And "the smile of God is over all."

Wisconsin Lumberman, 23 March 1864

---

[11] Final lines of "The Judgment" by Harry Vail, *Wisconsin Lumberman,* 16 March 1864, p. 1. This poem and the epigraph appeared the following week.

[12] The poem "Strangers Yet!" by Richard Monckton Milnes, Lord Houghton (1809-1885) had appeared in *Wisconsin Pinery,* 19 October 1860.

GO IN PEACE.

Go in peace, departing year; [13]
When thou art no longer here,
　　When I think of thee as dead,
All the ills that thou hast wrought me,
All the griefs that thou hast brought me,
　　Tears that thou hast bade me shed,
Tender ties thy hand hath riven,—
All shall be to thee forgiven—
　　　　Go in peace.

Though with every thought of thee
Mournful memories come to me,
　　Of that dark distressful hour,
When the angel in our home
Spread her spirit wings to roam,
　　Vanished from our longing sight;
Yet we know that she is blest—
No reproach shall break thy rest,—
　　　　Go in peace.

Neither am I all forsaken—
Thou hast given, as well as taken;
　　And another blue-eyed one
Smiles as *she* was wont to smile,
From a heart untouched by guile,
　　Murmurs in as sweet a tone.
Take for this, ere thou depart,
Blessings from a mother's heart,—
　　　　Go in peace.

31 December 1858
Wisconsin Pinery, 7 January 1859

---

[13] Published as "To The Old Year" in *Wisconsin Pinery*. The following note was included: "We welcome to the Poet's Corner once more our old and much esteemed, but too long hitherto absent favorite, Ada J. More [sic]. We trust she will for the future be more mindful of us and the pleasure with which we always hail her sweet numbers.—Ed."

The poets of life's mystery
  Have sung with tuneful art,
But could they trace the history
  Of a single human heart—
All its passions, hopes and fears,
All its trials, tumults, tears,
All its depth of ecstasy,
In the wild idolatry
  On some earthly idol shed,—
Every throbbing pulse of bliss,
  When the soul, too full for mirth,
Lies entranced in happiness,
  As the moonbeams bathe the earth,—
All its weight of agony,
  When the bright illusion's fled,
And beneath the wintry sky
  All the flowers of hope lie dead,—
Every wild and burning thought
Of the spirit tempest wrought.
Every sad despairing word,
Only by the night-stars heard,—
  Every tear-drop, every sigh,
All the spirit's weariness,
All the dark world's dreariness,
  Every longing wish to die,—
Oh! could these in verse be told,
With a truthful pen and bold,
Eyes would dim and cheeks grow pale
At the wild impassioned tale.
But the pen or voice may never
  All the heart's emotions tell,
And its deepest thoughts must ever—
Till the soul and body sever,
  In its own still chambers dwell.

Pine Cottage, 25 March 1856
Wisconsin Pinery, 7 April 1856
Milwaukee Daily Sentinel, 18 January 1861 as "Heart Mysteries"

MY GRAVES.

Upon the cold, cold snow I kneel,
   Beside my little graves,
My heart so cold I scarcely feel
   The wind that round me raves.
Here, side by side, my darlings rest,
   Amidst the wintry storm,
Who lately to a mother's breast
   Were folded close and warm.

And oh! were mine that strange belief,
   That with the body dies
The soul that loves, what floods of grief
   Would here o'erwhelm my eyes!
Ah, no! Their dust is precious still,
   Even as the robes they wore,
That bid the eye with tear-drops fill,
   Remembering "all is o'er."

But in the land of life and light
   Their happy spirits dwell,
With forms more fair, with smiles more bright,
   Than those we loved so well.
And oh! there is a blessed thought,
   That comes to soothe my pain,—
With such sweet comfort is it fraught,
   I will not deem it vain,—

My babes, with more than earthly charms,
   In dreaming hours I see,
Within my angel mother's arms
   Enfolded tenderly.
Their eyes in wondering innocence
   Look sweetly forth the while,
And He who called my dear ones hence,
   Upon them seems to smile.

Another form beside them stands—[14]
   The brother whom I mourn—
A golden lyre within his hands,
   His voice in praise upborne.
And Oh! this blessed dream hath power
   Naught else could e'er impart,
To cheer the sad and lonely hour,
   And soothe my wounded heart.

Wisconsin Pinery, 8 April 1859

---

[14] This final stanza appeared in the original 1859 publication of the poem, but not in *Under the Pines* (1875). Her brother Edward Read Hall (b. 1834) had died one month prior to the poem's first appearance on 8 March 1859. The graves are those of her daughter Mary Ada Phillips, who had died in September 1858, and her son Edwin Hall Phillips, who had died on 13 February 1859. Her "angel-mother," Mary Dascomb Hall, had died in 1836 at the age of 35. When she wrote this, she was pregnant with her daughter Florence and had one surviving child, four-year old John Henry Phillips, who would die the following February.

IN THE DEPTHS.

Down in the depths—
The deep and dreamy and sorrowful depths,
Weary and weak, and unable to rise,
Languidly lifting my longing eyes
Up to the heights—the glorious heights,
Whose clear-cut peaks, on the cloudless skies,
Glowing with light, and forever bright
With the smile of God, that knows no night,
Draw my soul upward! In vain! in vain!
Alas! for the burden! Alas! for the chain!

Down in the depths!
Yet the scenes of life go on around me,
   And I play my part, as an actor may,
While my soul, benumbed by the spell that has bound me,
   Grows fainter and wearier day by day,
And my eyes are dim that I scarce can see
The hands of my angels, that beckon to me
From the skies that bend the heights above,—
Yet I own—in my sorrowful heart—the love
That tenderly bore my darlings hence,
In the bloom of their sinless innocence.

"Out of the depths,"
Said one of old, "I have cried to Thee";[15]
And his prayer was answered. His soul, set free,
Mounted up to the heights of God,
And shed the songs of his joy abroad,
As the lark her music from Heaven's own gate.
Look up, faint heart! No spell of fate
Enthralls the holier spell of prayer,—
This amulet on thy bosom wear,
And the chain shall fall off thee, the burden grow light,
And thy step shall not falter ascending the height.

Wisconsin Lumberman, 20 October 1865

---

[15] Psalm 130:1.

ALONE.
(Translated from the French)[16]

Pray, love for me,—
    Ever, when night comes down,
I think of thee,—
    Alas! I am alone!

Pray for my weal
    To Him who reigns above;
Deeply I feel,
    His is a *father's* love.

Kneel at the shrine,—
    Thy life is good and pure;
May joy be thine!
    My lot is—*to endure.*

Pray, then, for me;
    Upon my knees I bow
Nightly, for thee;
    Love, for whom prayest thou?

Milwaukee Daily Sentinel, 16 March 1865

---

[16] Translation of a poem titled "*Toute Seule,*" published in the *Milwaukee Daily Sentinel,* 16 March 1865, with the following note: "The following little gem, which originally appeared in the *Home Journal,* under the signature of "Esperanza," is sent us by our valued contributor, Miss Ada J. Moore, with a translation by herself." It also appeared in the *Lumberman,* 24 March 1865. See the original in the Appendix.

UNDER THE STARS.

The summer night is calm and still;
  I stand alone beneath the stars,
And feel my soul within me thrill,
  Gazing like prisoner from his bars,
With an intense and yearning glance,
Upon creation's fair expanse.
  My heart stands still;
  Against my will
I linger in the dew-damp air,
And my whole being seems one earnest prayer;
A prayer *to know;* to find the hidden key
That shall unlock creation's mystery,
  And let the light in on my saddened mind,
That treads its destined path,
Where storms have spent their wrath,
  With tremulous footsteps, groping like the blind,
Yet leaning trustingly, for life or death,
Upon its only stay, the staff of Faith.
  Clouds gather o'er the sky
    In answer to my prayer
    Comes on the silent air
The soft night-wind that wanders through the pines;
Its voice unsyllabled my heart divines—
        It whispers "Wait!"
And I *must* wait for this,
  Until, ere long, night's breeze
Unfelt my brow shall kiss,
  When colder dews than these
Are gathering there—
Then shall be heard my prayer.

Wisconsin State Rights, 17 July 1861
Milwaukee Daily Sentinel, 6 September 1864 as "Aspirations"

LINES FOR THE TIMES.

By "No Matter Who."[17]

There's a certain class of people,
  In this sublunary sphere—
(And if I'm not mistaken,
  You'll find them even here),
Who think the rare old precept
  To the ancient Romans given,
And esteemed so full of wisdom
  That they deemed it came from Heaven,—

In this glorious age of progress
  Has become quite obsolete;
So they choose another motto,
  For these latter times more meet.
It is "Know thyself" no longer—
  So they say, and who can doubt them—
But "Mortal, know they neighbors,
  And everything about them!"

To attain this worthy object,
  All other cares forego;
To gain this glorious knowledge,
  You cannot stoop too low.
Heed not the ancient croakers,
  Who ask, with solemn phiz—
"Is it anybody's business
  What another's business is?"

No! we'll join the glorious party,
  That to giant size has grown,
To mind our neighbor's business
  And "Know Nothing" of our own.

---

[17] Published under the name, "No Matter Who," not Ada J. Moore. Reprinted 9 February 1932 in a letter to the editor of the *Stevens Point Journal* from an "Old Settler": "This selection from the book, "Under the Pines," by Ada J. Moore, nee Mrs. E. E. Phillips, is as true today as it was when it [was] written in 1875. It would have been equally true had it been recorded 1,900 years ago. Apparently, human nature does not change greatly in that space of time judging by books of old and personal observation today."

Hurrah! for the Rights of Meddlers!
    For the Freedom of our day!
For this glorious Age of Progress!
    And for Young America!

Stevens Point, May 1855
Wisconsin Pinery, 17 May 1855

Lightly tripping, often slipping,
  With her little arms outstretched,—
Gaily crowing, bright eyes glowing,
  When the wished-for aim is reached,—
Gravely sitting, with my knitting
  Growing "beautifully less,"—
Gently bitten by the kitten,
  For too loving a caress,—
That's our darling—
      Baby Florence.[18]

Creeping shyly, stealing slyly
  Round my chair when I am sewing,
All excited, and delighted,
  If the brisk "machine" is going,—
Fear of paining scarce restraining,
  In her eager, sportive zeal,
The small finger, raised to linger
  On the swiftly-turning wheel,—
That's our darling—
      Baby Florence.

Sweetly resting, yet still nesting
  Closer to my yearning breast,
Like some angel, child-evangel,
  Seems she in her holy rest.
He who knows how much we need her,
  To preserve us from despair—
Surely He will let us keep her,
  He will bid the Reaper spare
Our *one* darling—
      Baby Florence.

Wisconsin Pinery, 4 January 1861

---

[18] Florence Dascomb Phillips (1859-1918).

"AS GOOD AS EVER WERE CAUGHT."
A SONG. [19]

My sorrowful darling, come hither,—
   I'll whisper a word in thine ear:
Though the flowers of affection may wither,
   They'll blossom again next year;
Though life may seem empty to thee, love,
   Remember what we have been taught—
There's just as good fish in the sea, love,
   As ever by angler were caught!

Though deep is the sting and regretful,
   Love leaves when his gay flight is o'er,
Time renders the sad heart forgetful,
   And bids it to sorrow no more.
There's light in the future for thee, love,
   And joy will return, though unsought—
There's quite as good fish in the sea, love,
   As ever by angler were caught!

There's many a nobler and braver
   Than he who could blight a young heart;
Henceforth, though thy smile may be graver,
   Yet let it not wholly depart.
And when once more thy heart shall be free, love,
   Remember what we have been taught—
There's just as good fish in the sea, love,
   As ever by angler were caught!

July 1868

---

[19] Title is a line from the song "There are Plenty of Fish in the Sea" by Steven Foster.

Christian pastor, sent of God,
　Standing on the mountain-top,
Publishing His Word abroad,
　Let thine hands be lifted up.
Think not, in thy lofty sphere,
　That the heavenly heights are won;
Though their summits seem so near,
　Scarce the journey is begun.

Humble Christian, on the plain,
　Gazing up with longing view,
Scarcely hoping to attain,—
　Let thine hands be lifted too.
Press with holy courage on,
　Where the heights of Faith arise;
Bear the cross, and wear the crown,
　On the hills of Paradise.

Doubting Christian, in the vale,
　Where Despair's grim castle stands,
Let not heart and spirit fail—
Upward lift imploring hands.
Dwell not on the erring Past—
　Heaven a Future hath for thee;
Mount up boldly, and at last[20]
　Glorious thy reward shall be.

Milwaukee Daily Sentinel, 24 March 1869

---

[20] This line appears in the 1869 original but not in *Under the Pines.*

MEMORIES.

I sit alone in the moonlight,
  And gaze on the starry skies,
While the night-dews fall around me,
  And the earth in silence lies—
Save the rushing of the river,
  On its strong resistless way,
And the shrill and varied murmur
  Of the insect orchestra.

My babes are slumbering sweetly,
  And the household is at rest;
But a gushing tide of memories
  That are wakening in my breast,
And the charm of this glorious evening,
  Have banished repose from me,
And I sit and dream in the moonlight,
  As in days that have ceased to be.

There hangeth many a picture
  In the galleries of the Past,
Illumed by a fitful radiance,
  From the torch of Memory cast;
And I cannot choose but linger
  In these dim and shadowy halls,
And dream of the friends whose faces
  Look down from the pictured walls.

I am happy in the Present,
  And what is the Past to me,
With its lonely hours of sadness,
  Or its wild unthinking glee?
Strange, that the heart will linger,
  However Life's stream may flow,
With a vague mysterious yearning
  O'er the days of Long Ago.

Wisconsin Pinery, 8 October 1857 as "The Past"
Milwaukee Daily Sentinel, 2 September 1864 as "Memories"

LITTLE CARL.
BORN FEBRUARY 22, 1862.

Clasped in my arms the darling lies—
Upturned to mine his earnest eyes,
His tiny hand my cheek caressing,
In calm contentment, blessed and blessing.

No longer pale and wan and weak—
The hue of health is on his cheek;
A new life sparkles in his eye,
And rounds his form to symmetry.

Thank God—yet words are cold and weak
My full heart's grateful joy to speak;
A firmer faith and warmer zeal,
May these betoken what I feel.

My child, I breathe for thee one prayer:
If He who gave, thy life shall spare,
May it, in noble deeds, be worth,
The glory of thy day of birth.[21]

Milwaukee Daily Sentinel, 6 November 1862

---

21 Carl F. Phillips, d. 1894. The 1862 version concluded with two additional lines: "With many a tone / To mortal minstrelsy unknown," based on Lord Byron's 1816 poem, *The Siege of Corinth* ("And take a long-unmeasured tone, / To mortal minstrelsy unknown").

FAR AWAY.

Know ye where my eyes are straying,
    Yearningly, to-night?
Though I watch my children, playing,
    With my outward sight,
The eyes of my spirit are far away—
Ask me not where, lest I say thee nay.

Know ye what my voice is whisp'ring,[22]
    Lovingly, to-night?
Though I answer to their lisping,
    Cheerful words and light,
The voice of my spirit is far away—
Ask me not where, lest I say thee nay.

Know ye whom my heart is blessing,
    Tenderly, to-night?
Though I lavish fond caressing
    On each playful sprite,
My heart's best blessing is far away—
Ask me not where, lest I say thee nay.

Milwaukee Daily Sentinel, 19 March 1864

---

[22] In the original version, stanzas 2 and 3 are reversed.

BURIED SEED.[23]

In a sunny Alpine valley,
  Wrought a peasant at his toil,
Till the seed at length was hidden
  Underneath the furrowed soil.

Thankful that his task was ended,
  With a smile he viewed the field,
Dreaming of the golden harvest
  That the buried grain would yield.

On a sudden, from the mountains
  Echoed, far above his head,
Startling sounds, that every Switzer
  Learns to know with fear and dread.

Downward swept a mighty glacier,
  Thundering on from rock to rock,
And the peasant fled affrighted,
  While the earth beneath him shook.

Scarcely had his fleeting footsteps
  Time a safe retreat to gain,
Ere the huge ice-torrent, falling,
  Buried deep the smiling plain.

Homeward turned he sadly musing
  On his weary, fruitless toil;
Vain the hope of future harvest
  Springing from that icy soil.

Years passed on. The stalwart peasant
  Aged grew with toil and care,
Ere the suns of fleeting summers
  Left once more the valley bare.

---

[23] The poem was prefaced by a note to the editors: "In reading you brief article on the recent decision of the Supreme Court, I was so much impressed with the beautiful illustration which it contained, that I took the liberty of rendering it into verse, which is herewith placed at your disposal. A. J. M." The case she is referring to is probably Gillespie v. Palmer, in which the Wisconsin Supreme Court affirmed the right of black men to vote in Wisconsin.

Then his son—a rugged stripling—
  Led the oxen to the plain,
Once again to drive the plough-share
  Where the ice so long had lain.

But he met a sight of wonder!
  In the furrows, everywhere,
Tender blades of wheat were springing
  Upward to the sun and air!

And ere long a bounteous harvest
  Had been garnered from the sod,
'Midst whose sheaves the grateful peasant
  Sang *"Te Deums"* to his God.

Thus the germs of Truth, though buried
  Deep, while Fraud and Falsehood reign,
'Neath the broadening light of ages,
  Ever spring to life again—

Spring to life in rich fruition,
  Shaming prophecies of gloom,
While the voice of Faith, triumphant,
  Shouts the glorious "Harvest Home."[24]

Wisconsin State Journal, 12 April 1866

---

[24] Possibly a reference to the hymn "Come, Ye Thankful People, Come" by Henry Alford, 1844.

MY LOST JEWELS.
[Respectfully inscribed to Mrs. H. R. Warren.] [25]

I too had jewels given to my care—
Gems which I hope in Heaven, one day, to wear;
Still were they mine, our cottage hearth would be
Set with five pure and precious stones—ah, me!

First to my home a priceless diamond came, [26]
Sparkling with such a pure ethereal flame,
That, gazing on its radiance, half I wist,
Some star must from its heavenly home be missed.

Next came my pearl—a "pearl of price" to me, [27]
So pure and fair in its sweet symmetry.
I wore my diamond proudly on my breast,
But hid my pearl within my inner vest.

Ah! then no mortal was so blest as I,
My earth-held gaze no longer sought the sky;
When others passed whose jewels were less rare,
I pitied them, with self-complacent air.

Then a pale emerald, with lustre wan, [28]
Was added to my treasures, and yet none
More tenderly was cherished, while my gaze
Dwelt lovingly on its enfeebled rays.

Then came a stranger to my home by night,
And asked me for my sweet pearl as one whose right
Might not be questioned. Wildly to my breast
I clasped the treasure, dearer than the rest.

He took it from me—on my soul there fell
A gloomy darkness that no words can tell;
Yet I had treasures left—I lived for them,
And closer clasped my latest-given gem.

---

[25] Replying to the poem "Jewels" by Mrs. Helen R. Warren that had appeared in the *Daily Sentinel* on 22 November. Warren herself replied with "A Sister's Voice" on 18 February 1863.

[26] John Henry Phillips (1855-1860).

[27] Mary Ada Phillips (1857-1858).

[28] Edwin Hall Phillips (1858-1859).

He came again; with ruthless hand and cold
He tore the pale gem from my clinging hold.
Ah me! the empty hours, the lonely days—
Upward I sought in vain to lift my gaze.

But time passed on, another treasure came—
A glowing ruby with its lambent flame;[29]
And with my diamond sparkling on my breast,
I thought no more of that unwelcome guest.

But, ah! *he came!* Till then I had not known
How heavenly had my diamond's lustre grown;
I could not keep it from its native sky—
It was too pure a gift for such as I.

'T was a keen agony, but years are o'er—
May that grim guest our threshold cross no more!
God spare my crystal, with its tender light,[30]
My ruby, flushed with hues so warmly bright.

Milwaukee Daily Sentinel, 18 December 1862

---

[29] Florence Dascomb Phillips (1859-1918).

[30] Carl F. Phillips (1862-1894).

SEPTEMBER.

The day is cool and bright and clear—
   No dreamy mists o'erhang the sky,
No languid southern airs are here,
   With breath of fragrance floating by,—
And yet, I know not why, to-day
Something within me shrinks away
From every thought of care;
I long, unseen, to wander where
No sight or sound of toil may come,
Save the wild-bee's drowsy hum;
In some dim and shadowy wood—
Some fairy-haunted solitude—
Where the forest blooms are springing,
And the perfumed air is bringing
Rest to the over-wearied brain—
Rest from care, relief from pain;
There to sit and idly dream
   Of the unreturning Past,
While the stream, with changing gleam,
   Murmurs, "Can the Present last?"
Murmurs vainly, to an ear
Predetermined not to hear,
Like the Lotus-eaters olden,
Lying where the sands were golden,
With a magic spell o'ercome,
Willingly forgetful of their island home.
Vain are these Utopias—
   Dreaming hours are sweet,
Yet they strengthen not our souls
   Cares and griefs to meet.
Life is full of solemn truth;
Fair as were the dreams of youth,
Time has laid them in the grave,
With some lovelier things he gave;
There, in silence, let them dwell,
While with wrung hearts, we murmur "It is well!"

Wisconsin State Rights, 9 October 1861
Milwaukee Daily Sentinel, 22 September 1869 as "Utopias"

Sitting, on this April day,
  With the burial grove in sight,
Where three little forms of clay
  Slumber through a dreamless night,—

While my happy little Floy,
  Full of springtime joy and mirth,
Chases Carl, the laughing boy,
  Near the consecrated earth,—

Thinking, Were they yet alive,
  Frolicsome and gay as these!
Were they *all* at play—the five,
  And no graves beneath the trees!

He, my noble, gifted boy,
  With the soul-light in his eye,
Who, in earth's first dawn of joy,
  Looked up, wistful, to the sky.

And the soft-eyed angel girl,
  Fairer than white lilies are—
Tender names we called her—Pearl
  Fittest seemed for her to wear.

And the babe, with pale, meek brow,
  Whose short life was full of pain—
Nay, I see my madness now,
  Could I wish *him* here again?

Would I, selfishly forgetful,
  Call my angels from their bliss?
Could I bear their eyes regretful,
  Wakening from that world to this?

This, where naught is sweet but love,
  And where love too oft deceives,
Where in Spring our footsteps move
  Over last year's withered leaves.

Nay! beside their graves I kneel—
    Let the sun the clouds dispel,
While I murmur—as I feel—
    God, Thou hast done all things well.

Wisconsin State Journal, 28 April 1864

MOUNT MANSFIELD.[31]

"Alone with Nature!" On this mossy bank
I seat myself to spend a quiet hour,
Bidding all restless anxious thoughts give way,
And let the grandeur of this glorious scene
Find entrance in my soul.

                Around me rise
The "hills of God," the wooded mountain tops,
In silent majesty. Before me stands
The peerless Mansfield, with its profile vast
Uplifted to the sky. Thus might, of old,
Some giant Titan look, when laid at rest
On Pelion's heights, in calm and conscious strength.
The snows of winter, like a hoary beard,
Are lingering on his massive lips and chin,
Despite the smiles of sweet and sunny June.
Silent and awed I sit, beneath the spell
Of his vast presence, as a pilgrim bows
Before the shrine to which his weary feet
Have made their wonted pilgrimage.
                      And yet, even here,
My thoughts turn backward to a quiet home
Far in the sunny West, beneath whose oaks
My boy's glad shout is ringing; on whose porch
My blue-eyed darling, in her father's arms,[32]
Watches the sunset, and in infant glee,
With prattling voice beguiles his lonely heart.
One hour with them were dearer far to me,
Than years to gaze upon this glorious scene,
In unshared solitude.

                From thee I turn,
O slumbering giant, with a calm farewell.

---

[31] Near Stowe, Vermont. This mountain resembles a long human face in profile. The poem appeared in *Milwaukee Daily Sentinel*, 15 June 1867, and *The Wisconsin Lumberman*, 21 June 1867, with this introduction: "The following excellent poem, full of sublimity and beauty, we clip from the Milwaukee *Daily Sentinel*. It was written by Mrs. Dr. Phillips, of this city, who is now on a visit to Vermont, her native State."

[32] The boy is Carl and the infant is Ellen "Nellie" C. Phillips (April 1867 - September 1867).

And yet, if I may be so blest, once more
To sit at sunset in my peaceful home,
Lulling my babe to rest,—thine outline vast
Shall rise full oft upon the amber skies
In vivid imagery, and I shall seem
Once more to sit upon this flowery bank,
And gaze upon thy grandeur.
                         Thus, to me,
Thy memory dearer than thyself shall be.

Stowe, Vermont, 2 June 1867

Moonlight softly glorious
   Slumbers on the snow—
Ah! what thoughts steal o'er us,
   With its mystic glow!
What memories of the by-gone years—
Too sad for mirth, too sweet for tears—
'Neath the magic spell awake.
Let no sound the stillness break—
Let me sit and muse and dream.
Thus the moon was wont to gleam
   On the snowy mountains
      That my childhood knew,
   And their ice-bound fountains
      Glistened in my view,
Fair as yonder lake, that seems
All one flood of molten beams.
Dreamed I then of what should be
In the Future, that for me
Waited in the distant West,
Love the sacred, Love the blest—
   Childhood's sweet caressings,
      In a home of bliss?
   Nay, midst all my guessings,
      Never guessed I this.

Madison, 23 January 1864
Wisconsin Lumberman, 3 February 1864

Little Maud, among the clover,
  In a little cottage dwelt;
Mother had she none to love her,
Yet an angel bent above her,
  When at evening prayer she knelt.

And a consciousness of blessing
  Softly through the twilight fell,
Sweeter than the fond caressing,
When a mother's hand is pressing
  Ringlets that she loves so well.

Through the darkness and the dawning,
  While the little dreamer slept,—
Through the brightness of the morning,
Like a charm her soul adorning,
  Little Maud this treasure kept.

And its sweetness lingered o'er her
  All the long and weary day;
Pleasant visions thronged before her,
And the hate that others bore her
  Vanished in its light away.

Thus she grew so meek and holy,
  That her life was like a dream!
Vision-like, it faded slowly,
Ere it vanished from us wholly,
  Like the twilight's fading gleam.

April 1868

---

[33] Published without attribution in *The Daily Evening Express* [Lancaster, PA], 2 April 1868.

A MEMORY.

Is this the sweetest of all summer eves,
Made up of moonlight, music and green leaves?
Nay, in my youth I knew an eve as fair,
A scene of moon-lit loveliness as rare.

Its beauty drew me from my cottage home,
Yet suffered not my restless feet to roam;
Entranced, I leaned upon the rustic gate,
And questioned of the night my future fate.

The stars were silent, but the tall elm trees
Bent low their heads and whispered to the breeze;
Ah! mystic oracles of night! that still
The dreamer's heart interprets as it will.

I knew not then the night's despairing tone
Was but the wild, weird echo of my own,
And bowed my head, with scarce a ray of hope,
To Fancy's darkly-tinted horoscope.

Thank God, those oracles, if read aright,
Had been as bright and peaceful as the night;
Than mine this moonlight gilds with amber rays,
No happier home, or heart more full of praise.

Milwaukee Daily Sentinel, 8 August 1867

AN INVOCATION.

Why art thou still delaying,
    O Sunny Spring?
Where are thy footsteps straying?
    O haste, and bring
The balmy dews and gentle showers,
And wreathe thy brow with early flowers.

Our spirits have longed for thy coming—
    As never before;
To hear the wild-bee's humming
    In the field once more,—
To breathe the soft and dewy air
That thrills us like a silent prayer.

How can our hearts be cheery,
    Our spirits glad,
When our mother earth is dreary,
    In russet clad,
And all her parched fields wait in vain
The coming of the welcome rain?

Then hasten, O beautiful maiden—
    Queen of the year,
With the wealth of the spring-time laden—
    Our hearts to cheer,
With springing flowers of beauty rare,
And soft, life-breathing, balmy air.

Milwaukee Daily Sentinel, 4 May 1872

UNDER THE OAKS.

Under the oaks I linger to-night,
  Though the dews are falling round me,
For the moon's soft beams, with their mystical gleams,
  In reverie's chains have bound me.

'T is a night for memory's siren song
  Of the past with its checkered story;
Yet the present is sweet, and its hours are fleet,
  And the night is full of glory.

Let me dream awhile as I used to dream,
  Of wild romantic blisses,
And forget, if I may, the mingling of gray,
  With the brown of my childhood's tresses.

'T is seldom I yield to a mood like this,
  Or cherish a thought regretful;
But the charm of a night so wondrously bright
  Makes the heart of its duties forgetful.

And under the oaks I linger still,
  While all that I love are sleeping
In a beautiful dream, 'neath the moonlight's gleam,
  And the night-dews softly weeping.

Stevens Point, 7 July 1870
Milwaukee Daily Sentinel, 20 July 1870

When the heart is full of rapture,
  Of unutterable bliss,
And the earth-born spirit trembles
  At its own wild happiness—
When the cheek is flushed and burning,
  And the pulses throbbing high,
And the heart's unspoken secret
  Sparkles in the soul-lit eye,—

From the din of crowds retreating,
  Nature's peaceful haunts we seek,
Where her soft and cooling breezes
  Gently fan the fevered cheek;
Where no sight or sound unwelcome
  Breaks our blissful reverie,—
While all nature smiles around us
  With a gladsome sympathy.

And when love and joy have vanished,
  With their sunlight, from the heart,
Shrouding all our life in darkness,
  That may never more depart;
When the soul is faint and weary
  With earth's care and strife and gloom,
And the only beam that shineth,
  Gilds the pathway to the tomb,—

Shrinking like the pale mimosa,
  From officious voice and eye,
Oft we wander, in our anguish,
  Where the green-wood shadows lie,—
There to kneel with aching temples,
  On the soft cool mosses pressed,
All our wild despair outpouring,
  As upon a mother's breast.

And the low melodious murmur
  Breathing from the wind-swept pine,
Seems a gentle voice of pity,

From some visitant divine,
While the soothing tear-drops, gushing
    From the long unmoistened eye,
Tell how sweet to stricken spirits,
    Nature's gentle ministry.

Wisconsin Pinery, 24 July 1856

APRIL.

Can this be the maiden fair,
  Known through all the bygone years
For her soft and melting air,
  Sunny smiles and sparkling tears?

Now, so cold and stony-hearted,
  Not a tear bedews her cheek;
All her winsomeness departed—
  Even her smiles are cold and bleak.

Winter, with his icy trident,
  Holds her in his bondage fell,
And no charm, howe'er so potent,
  Can release her from the spell.

Haste thee, April—hast away,
  In thy strangely altered guise;
Let us greet the gladsome May,
  With the sunlight in her eyes.

Milwaukee Daily Sentinel, 29 April 1874

STRENGTH IN SUFFERING.

"Be patient in a world like this.
  And thou shalt know ere long—
Know how sublime a thing it is
  To suffer and be strong."

LONGFELLOW[34]

O words beyond all praise!
  O noble poet heart!
That with thy soul-inspiring lays
  Such comfort canst impart!
Far down the stream of Time—
  From thine immortal song,
Sad hearts shall learn the art sublime—
  "To suffer and be strong."

'T is sweet to know on earth
  The tender bliss of love,—
To lean upon a heart whose worth
  The years alone can prove;
But if Life's star has set
  Beneath Oblivion's wave,—
If those who once have loved, forget,
  Or slumber in the grave,—

If hearts that should have beat
  With but one pulse together,
Drift wide apart, no more to meet,
  Like ships in stormy weather,—
If brows that throb with pain,
  No tender kisses press,
And no fond arm the form sustain,
  That faints with weariness,—

It is a bitter cup—
  Yet let the sufferer rise,
And on these griefs, like stairs, mount up,

---

[34] Epigraph is from "The Light of Stars" (1839) by Henry Wadsworth Longfellow. The first line
was "O fear not in a world like this" in Longfellow's original.

Unfaltering, to the skies.
What though the path be hard,
    Starless the night, and long?
How blest at last is their reward
    Who suffer and are strong.

Milwaukee Daily Sentinel, 20 February 1861
Wisconsin Lumberman, 2 December 1864

AUGUST.

The Summer is passing by,
  The roses of May and June
Are faded, and there seems a half-breathed sigh
  In the rivulet's merry tune.
The sigh will grow more deep,
And the gayer flowers will sleep,
And a chastening shadow creep,
  O'er the summer's glory soon.

What will the Autumn bring?
  I ask, with a trembling heart;
'Midst its fruitful store, *one* precious thing
  I seek; must my hope depart?
Must the same dark shadow come
  O'er the sunlight of our home,
That blighteth the Summer's bloom
  With its silent, fateful art?

Angel of Death and Decay!
  Breathe on the flowers, if thou must!
But oh! seek not in smiling homes thy prey,
  Smiting fond hopes to dust!
For the roses on the plain
  Shall revive with the April rain,
But the dead come not again
  To the hearts that love and trust.

Milwaukee Daily Sentinel, 22 August 1866

THE WIFE'S VIGIL.
[Suggested by a Picture.]

A woman by her fireside;
      Who can tell
The thoughts that in her bosom
      Surge and swell,
As she sits alone by the dying fire,
Vacantly watching the sparks expire.

She has hushed the weary children
      To their rest,
Putting aside the sorrows
      Of her breast;
Now is her hour to watch and weep—
Oh! the vigils that women keep!

Her thoughts are of the absent;
      What recks he—
Among his boon companions
      Wild and free—
What cares he for the yearning grief
That finds in tears its only relief?

Weep on—'t is the lot of women,
      One and all;
From the eyes of the happiest, even—
      Tears must fall.
We sit at home, and we dream and doubt,
And cherish fears of we know not what.

'T is best to be calm and hopeful—
      Love and trust;
And if our earthly idols
      Fall to dust,
We have still the hope of that heavenly day
When all tears shall be wiped away.

Milwaukee Daily Sentinel, 13 December 1862

TO "LA PETITE."

Welcome, little waif of being,[35]
  Wafted from the unknown shore,
Rest, within my arms enfolded,
  Now thine earthward flight is o'er.

Lying thus upon my bosom,
  With thy velvet cheek to mine,
Like a rosebud, half in blossom,
  Seems that tiny face of thine.

Sinks my heart, as I caress it,
  Lest it never come to fruit—
Many a rosebud in my garden
  Has been blighted at the root.

Yet I clasp thee just as fondly,
  And I cannot love thee less,
And thy dark eyes seem to answer,
  Trustingly, my warm caress.

In their depths a prayer is imaged,
  Joining it, my heart goes forth—
Part us not, O gracious Father,
  Until *one* shall tire of earth.

Stevens Point, July 1868
Milwaukee Daily Sentinel, 3 September 1868

---

[35] Possibly an unnamed child born between Nellie (1867) and Hattie May (1869) who died very soon after birth.

MAY FLOWERS.

Lightly fall the April showers,
Wooing forth the sweet May flowers
From their dreary tomb;
      Happy flowers,
Rescued from a night of gloom.

Timidly, amid the moss
Which their tangled fibres cross,
Fragrant May buds rise,
      And the children
Pluck them with a sweet surprise.

At the foot of some brown hill,
Where the snowbanks linger still,
Violets peep forth.
      Smiling brightly
At the cold blasts from the North.

Ah! no blossoms are so dear,
In the summer of the year,
Midst the rosy bowers;
      First and fairest
Are the timid, sweet May flowers.

Wisconsin Lumberman, 20 April 1864

NELLIE.

IN AUGUST

Nellie's asleep—one soft hand pressing[36]
  Her cheek with a sweet *abandon*—
Ah! when I watch thee thus, my blessing,
  I know not if earth I stand on,
Or if thou and I have been borne away
To the fairy isles of sunny May,
  That in dreams the poets laud on.

Nellie's awake—from her sleep upspringing,
  With a laugh of infant gladness,
Her fair fond arms around me flinging,
  And my joy is touched with sadness,
Thinking, if I were no longer here,
  Where is the heart that would hold thee as dear,
Clasp thee with fondness as clinging?

IN SEPTEMBER

Nellie's asleep—but a shroud enfolds her,
  And her brow has an icy chillness,
Our eyes through dimming tears behold her,
  And our hearts beat loud in the stillness.
Calmly she lies, and strangely fair,
Wearing the smile she was wont to wear—
  Albeit a coffin holds her.

Nellie's awake—on her Savior's bosom,
  Gazing with wonder and gladness
On the heavenly flowers that around her blossom—
  Let her bliss rebuke our sadness.
Not a mother's breast, had she lingered here,
Could shield her as safely or hold her as dear,
  As the tender Heart she lies on.

Milwaukee Daily Sentinel, 10 October 1867
Wisconsin Lumberman, 25 October 1867

---

[36] Nellie is Ellen Cecilia Phillips who was born in April 1867. The original title was "Nellie's Asleep." This version contains significant revisions: the original first stanza was deleted and the current second stanza was added.

WHEREFORE?

In every haunt of sin and crime,
   Neglected children dwell,
Whose faces, old before their time,
   A saddening story tell;
While to a thousand happy homes,
   As to this home of ours,
With stealthy step, the reaper comes
   And culls the fairest flowers.
Wherefore? It is His will;
   O murmuring heart, be still!

Within the dismal mine,
   In cellars drear and cold,
Where sunbeams cannot shine,
   And walls are damp with mold,—
Young faces, pale and sad,
   Pine on from year to year,
While those with rosy health were glad
   Who dwell no longer here.
Wherefore? It is His will;
   O murmuring heart, be still!

The orphaned, homeless one
   Who knows not warmth or rest—
Who gladly would lie down
   On his dead mother's breast,
Lives on in want and woe,
   While from the sheltering heart,
The tenderest love that earth may know,
   Our cherished ones depart.
Wherefore? It is His will;
Believe and trust Him still!

Milwaukee Daily Sentinel, 18 December 1867

Why wakest thou, why weepest thou?
       Sorrow is unlovely.
"I wake at night—at night I weep,
When other eyes are closed in sleep,
When hearts that reck not of my sorrow
Are dreaming of a happy morrow.
I grieve not them, I grieve not thee,
Weeping at night, and silently."

Why wakest thou, why weepest thou?
       Sorrow is unfruitful.
"Not so; the eyes that never weep,
But calmly, coldly, wake and sleep,
Can never pierce with vision clear
The mysteries of this mortal sphere.
I harm not them, I harm not thee,
Weeping at night, and silently."

Why wakest thou, why weepest thou?
       Sorrow is ungrateful.
"Nay, to the blessings of my lot
My heart responds with grateful thought;
I know that many 'neath the sky
Have greater cause to weep than I.
I wrong not them, I wrong not thee,
Weeping at night, and silently."

DECEMBER.

Here's a welcome to thee, Winter!
  I joy to see thee come;
To hear old Boreas blustering loud,
  Around my pleasant home.

I share the children's rapture,
  When first the feathery snow
Comes floating lightly down to earth—
  The purest thing I know.

To me no summer landscape
  Can seem so fair and bright,
As when the brown bare oaks put on
  Their robes of stainless white.

If I regret my childhood,
  'T is not in sunny weather,
When violets bloom in every nook,
  For these I still can gather.

But when the happy children,
  With glowing cheeks and eyes,
Are coasting down the icy hill,
  With loud, exultant cries,—

Or when beneath the moonlight
  The graceful skaters glide,
And youthful hearts are throbbing high
  With mingled mirth and pride.

These joys for me are ended—
  Yet I murmur not at this,
In the warmth of my pleasant fireside joys,
  And my blue-eyed baby's kiss.

Milwaukee Daily Sentinel, 9 June 1869

HATTIE MAY.

Of all the winsome treasures
   That our dwelling have supplied
With a joy that far outmeasures
   Every earthly joy beside,
The brightest and the gayest,
   Through all the livelong day,
Is our roguish little Hattie—
   Our darling Hattie May.[37]

With her wavy golden tresses,
   And her sparkling eyes of blue,
With her clinging, sweet caresses,
   Bringing gladness ever new,
With her feet so lightly dancing,
   At the sound of music gay—
Nothing can be half so lovely
   As our darling Hattie May.

Though we mourn for those departed—
   Feeling painfully bereft—
We can scarce be broken-hearted,
   With so many treasures left;
And we pray that God will spare us—
   For many and many a day—
Our winsome little darling,
   Our blue-eyed Hattie May.

Milwaukee Daily Sentinel, 28 October 1869

---

[37] Harriet "Hattie" May Phillips (1869-1962).

THE SNOW BLOCKADE.[38]

Surely we all have been dreaming—
  Dreaming so soundly by night,
That the fairies have borne us northward,
  In a swift unconscious flight.

Have they left us in Alaska,
  Or in frozen Labrador?
Or are these the plains of Norway,
  In the kingdom of ancient Thor?

N'importe! We are here together,
  In our bright and cheerful home;
Father and mother and children,
  So let the tempest come!

Let old Boreas, with his cohorts,
  Entrench himself in might;
Build a glacial world around us,
  And shut the world from sight—

Shut out all strife and turmoil,
  All worldly cares and fears;
Shut in fond hearts, united
  By the tender ties of years.

In happy home communion
  Shall the swift-winged hours be spent,
While the sound of the raging tempest
  But heightens our sweet content.

And the only sigh we utter,
  As the day-beams slowly fade,
Is a sigh for the poor and homeless,
  In the days of the snow blockade.

Stevens Point, 15 March 1870
Milwaukee Daily Sentinel, 24 March 1870

---

[38] Reprinted in the *Stevens Point Journal*, 19 January 1932, in a letter to the editor from "Old Settler" titled, "A Snow Blockade as Described in 1875." According to *The New York Times*, 16 March 1870, "Another heavy snowstorm has prevailed all over the North-west since yesterday [March 14], and the trains are more or less blockaded. It is estimated in Minnesota that the snow is three feet deep on a level and about two feet deep in Wisconsin."

LINES SUGGESTED BY "BURIED LOVES."

Six times in love! Ah! well-a-day,[39]
And yet the hair not tinged with gray!
'T is plain man's love's a different thing from woman's,
A lucky circumstance for lordly humans.

Although, like Antony, they boast—
'All for love, and the world well lost,'[40]
Yet did it never strike your comprehension
That "all" is capable of much extension?

If man but loved as woman loves—
Whose every thought and impulse moves
Obedient to one all-absorbing passion—
Flirtations would not be so much in fashion.

"But women flirt"—'t is true, my friend,
And yet my sex I would defend;
Who knows what deep affections unrequited—
What tender home devotion worse than slighted—

Have driven them to such a course,
If not, indeed, to one far worse?
Give them but love for love, and few would ever,
With their own hands, those bonds so sacred sever.

Milwaukee Daily Sentinel, 11 September 1863

---

[39] She is responding to a poem by F. C. Long, published on August 26.

[40] Reference to John Dryden's play *All for Love; Or, The World Well Lost* (1677) based on the Antony and Cleopatra story.

You, my friend, esteem it better,
  Single life than wedded care,
By yourself to stand with firmness,
  Than another's lot to share;
And you challenge me to prove it,
  If there's wisdom in *my* choice.
Listen, then, this tranquil evening,
  To my sprit's musing voice.

Once my heart was cold as thine is,
  Girlish fancies all were o'er,
And in gazing down the future,
  Voices whispered, "Nevermore!"
Then I answered calmly, boldly,
  "I can tread life's path alone;"
And I sought to crush the longing
  For a heart to meet my own.

Through the years this might have lasted,
  And my life, perchance, had been
Like a tranquil river, gliding
  Through the meadows fair and green;
Yet at times, in narrow defiles,
  Where no prying eye might be,
Would the waves have lashed each other,
  Like the restless yearning sea.

But not thus my fate was written;
  As the slow hours circled by,
Rose the crescent moon of promise,
  In my dim and misty sky;
Slowly woke my doubting spirit
  To a knowledge of its bliss,
But all doubts and fears were banished
  By the fervent marriage kiss.

Not for you, the lonely-hearted,
  You whose highest joy is peace,
Will I paint those joys elysian—

Clothe in words the wordless bliss
Of the days and months that followed,
  When my spirit, once so cold,
Glowed with love beyond expression—
  Thrilled with happiness untold.

Scarcely could such glowing raptures
  Last through all the coming years,
Through a mother's pangs and trials,
  Weary hours and anxious fears;
But a deep, abiding gladness,
  Trusting love, devoid of art,
Tender sympathy, so precious
  To a woman's yearning heart—

These are mine—in joy or sorrow,
  And I count it better so,
Than to bear alone in silence
  All the griefs that women know;
For no lot is free from shadows,
  And to lone hearts they must be
Chill, like that the iceberg casteth
  On the dreary, frozen sea.

There is music in my dwelling—
  Childish laughter, ringing clear,
And the tiny, pattering footsteps—
  To a mother's heart so dear;
Loving arms are twined around me,
  Rosy lips to mine are pressed—
Oh! you dream not of the rapture
  Which can thrill a mother's breast!

True, my heart has known the anguish
  Only parent hearts can know—
When my first-born and my fairest
  Melted from me like the snow;
But 't is only those who suffer,
  Know how sweet the thought can be,
Of an angel child in Heaven,
  Saved from sin, from sorrow free.

In the annals of the future,
   If my lot be bliss or woe,
Health and joy, or pain and anguish,
   Know I not,—nor would I know;
But I seek no prouder title,
   And I ask no happier life,
Than of fond, devoted mother,
   And of loved and loving wife.

AFTER THE RAIN.

How strangely still this August day!
My prattling baby, tired of play,[41]
Upon the floor has sunk to sleep,
And lovingly my watch I keep,
Above her slumbers calm and deep.

The summer air is soft and warm—
Sweeter and purer for the storm;
As down the garden walks I gaze,
The flowers their drooping heads upraise,
With freshened hues and brighter rays.

A fairer flower my darling seems,
As on her hair the sunlight gleams;
Her cheek is softer than the rose,
And with a richer crimson glows,
As graceful is her light repose.

A mirthful thought disturbs her sleep;
Smile on—'t is better than to weep.
Whate'er may be thy fancied bliss—
Of promised toy, or mother's kiss,
We know it can be naught amiss.

Long may this guilelessness endure—
Thy visions ever be as pure;
Still may thy cheek its blush retain,
Thy tears be only those of pain,
Thy smiles like sunshine after rain.

Stevens Point, 23 August 1870
Milwaukee Daily Sentinel, 3 September 1870

---

[41] One-year-old Hattie May Phillips (1869-1962).

Ah, love! do you remember—
  'T was not so long ago,—
That evening in December,
  When brightly gleamed the snow?
When you and I went coasting—
  You had not learned to skate—
And my proud heart was boasting
  That I had "met my fate."

Our runners were the fleetest—
  We distanced all the rest;
Those moments were the sweetest
  That e'er my life have blest.
Alas! that in the freshness
  Of love's delirium sweet,
I won you, in my rashness,
  To try that desperate feat

The bank was steep before us—
  We stood upon its edge,
The starry sky was o'er us,
  Beneath, a snow-bound ledge;
With one wild shout of gladness,
  Together—side by side,
In brief but blissful madness,
  The long descent we tried.

I need not tell the sequel
  Of that appalling flight;
No words of mine can equal
  The horrors of that night!
I saved you—but forever
  A useless arm I bear;
In battle I may never
  Our country's colors wear.

Alas! a sadder story
  Is traced upon my heart;
For loss of fame or glory

These tear-drops do not start.
I love you as I loved you
    On that December night,
Though time, alas! hath proved you
    Inconstant, vain and light.

Last eve by chance I met you—
    Your smile was calm and cold;
'T were folly to regret you,
    Yet I am growing old,
And I recall with sadness,
    That time can ne'er abate,
That hour of youthful madness
    When I truly "met my fate."

Milwaukee Daily Sentinel, 11 April 1867

ON THE OCCASION OF A SILVER WEDDING.

Upon this festal night, [42]
When every heart is light,
May yours, my friends, be lighter still,
    And we, who fain your hand would clasp,
    In friendship's firm and cordial grasp,
Shall feel, even here, an answering thrill.

    Wedded in heart and hand,
    On midway heights ye stand,
And count the silver-shining years
    Adown the gentle slope of Time,
    Since rang in youth your wedding chime—
That sweetest "music of the spheres;"

    Perchance one tear ye shed,
    O'er hopes and pleasures fled,
Whose dirge rings sadly on the ear;
    Yet gratefully ye number o'er,
    Like gems, the rich and priceless store
Of joys and honors thronging every year.

    Before your lifted eyes
    Still loftier heights arise,
Whose summits glow with *golden* light.
    That ye, with hearts that truly blend,
    May, side by side, those heights ascend—
This wish shall crown your festal night.

February 1874

---

[42] Likely referring to the 25th wedding anniversary of Mr. and Mrs. T. H. McDill (*Stevens Point Journal,* 14 February 1874).

I am bringing thee, my love,
  Glad and joyous greeting;
With the children at my side,
  Home's dear band completing,
While thy faithful hand we grasp
In a warm and tender clasp.
Hark! the morning bells are ringing—
  Merry Christmas! Merry Christmas!
In glad echo to our singing—
  Merry Christmas! Merry Christmas!

Some are "gone before," my love—
  Fairest of our number,
Yet we would not waken them
  From their peaceful slumber;
Let not memory make us sad,
Let our hearts to-day be glad.
Hark! the morning bells are ringing—
  Merry Christmas! Merry Christmas!
In glad echo to our singing—
  Merry Christmas! Merry Christmas!

Every passing year, my love,
  Draws our spirits nearer,
And the sunlight of our home
  Groweth ever clearer,
For we know, whate'er befall,
Love can strengthen us through all.
Hark! the morning bells are ringing—
  Merry Christmas! Merry Christmas!
In glad echo to our singing—
  Merry Christmas! Merry Christmas!

ASPIRATIONS.

To the holy, pure and true,
    I aspire,
Lifting up my longing view,
    With desire
To be free from every stain,
    Earth-impressed;
Not released from care and pain,
    Yet most blest.

Blest in being raised above
    Soil and mire,
As the fleecy cloudlets move
    Ever higher,
Floating in the radiance bright,
    Thus would I
Dwell forever in the light,
    Pure and high.

Yet perchance I may have erred—
    Now and then,
Feeling all my spirit stirred
    From within,
By a smoothly ribald jest,
    Or the flow
Of pretended wit, at best
  Coarse and low;

Erred in this—that silent scorn
    Filled my thought,
Not the grief, of pity born,
    Christ has taught.
Like our Lord in this to be,
    I desire;
Unto this pure charity
    I aspire.

Milwaukee Daily Sentinel, 3 April 1866

DESPONDENCY.

Sunk in depths of worldliness,
Bound by circumstance and place,
Still unto lofty heights my soul aspires;
Brief flashes, leaping up from smouldering fires,
Deep buried, yet not dead—
Thank God, not wholly dead.

When these welcome flashes beam,
Wak'ning me from earth's vain dream,
Then seem my spirit's chambers all aglow,
And full of yearning thoughts that upward flow,
To God, and good, and Heaven—
Freedom from sin, in Heaven.

Then I long to write or speak
Earnest words to aid the weak;
To rouse the souls that sleep as mine has slept,
To cheer the eyes that weep as mine have wept,
For sorrow and for sin—
Most bitterly for sin.

But ah! the world, awhile forgot,
Resumes its empire o'er my thought;
The flames sink down, and all my soul is dark,
Lit only by one faintly glimmering spark,
Just ready to expire—
God! Let it not expire!

Madison, 15 February 1864
Wisconsin State Journal, 17 February 1864 as "Aspirations"

What shall we call our little pearl? [43]
The tiniest, fairest, baby-girl
That ever nestled in our arms
With all her sweet unconscious charms.

What name can be so soft and sweet,
For such a tiny stranger meet?
And fitted quaintly to express
Our darling's winsome helplessness?

No queenly name will do for thee,
Sweet atom of humanity;
Thou couldst not bear the burden, sure,
That royal babies must endure.

No classic appellation proud,
To thee can fitly be allowed;
No stately and patrician name,
A fairy elf like thee should claim.

One name there is, pure, soft and sweet,
And for our darling doubly meet.
Our tiny, precious, baby-girl—
Shall we not call thee *little Pearl?*

Stevens Point, July 1874
Milwaukee Daily Sentinel, 25 July 1874

---

[43] Pearl Estelle Phillips died on 24 July 1874, the day before this poem was published.

Into the Valley of Death
  Went I with trembling feet,
Hoping, and yearning, and praying,
  For the boon that I there might meet.
Dark—how dark! was the valley,
  And with terror my soul was stirred,
But my own low moans of anguish
  Were the only sounds I heard.

Up from the Valley of Death
  Came I with footsteps light,
Bearing the precious treasure,
  That I found in that dreary night.
Fair, how fair, was my darling,
  Lovely, my baby girl, [44]
And the tenderest names we called her—
  Rosebud, lily and pearl.

Back to the Valley of Death,
  Quickly my darling fled,
Ere she could know that I loved her,
  Or care for the tears I shed.
Glad, how glad, were the angels,
  Sweet was their welcome song;
So sweet that I heard its echo,
  Nor wept for my darling long.

August 1874
Milwaukee Daily Sentinel, 29 August 1874

---

[44] Pearl Estelle Phillips.

A WELCOME.

Thou art come, O fair May-maiden—
   Lovelier than we e'er beheld thee,
Both thine hands with garlands laden,
   Crowned with leafy vines that veiled thee,
Lest the Sun's enamored gaze
Linger on thy blushing face.

Holy May, thine early dawning
   Thrills us with a joy divine,
Since upon this sacred morning
   Doth thy new-born radiance shine,
And we lose all earthly cares
In the smile that Nature wears.

See the orchard, robed to meet thee,
   In a gala dress of white;
Crocuses and pansies greet thee,
   Iris, rich with purple light,
And the sweet anemone
Lifts her head to welcome thee.

Ah! with what a tender sadness,
   We whose locks are growing gray,
Now recall the spring-time gladness
   When our life was in its May;
When we plucked the earliest flowers,
Never joy could be like ours.

Now our children, merry-hearted,
   Gather May-buds on the plain,
And the joys, so long departed,
   In their young hearts live again.
Let the sunlight in their eyes
Smile away our secret sighs.

Stevens Point, 1 May 1870
Milwaukee Daily Sentinel, 21 May 1870

THE CONVALESCENT.

The weary hours of illness o'er,
  Again the garden paths I tread;
Was ever earth so fair before?
  So blue the skies above my head?

The flowerets wear a brighter hue,
  The trees in richest green are drest,
A sweeter song than e'er I knew,
  Swells from the robin's joyous breast.

And if the scene be passing fair
  When shines the golden light of day,
What words can paint its beauty rare,
  Beneath the moonbeams sliver ray?

The snow-ball, with its clustering bloom,
  Stands like a spirit robed in white;
The lilacs breathe their soft perfume
  Upon the dewy air of night.

The oaks, beneath the mystic spell
  Of night, are silent as the tomb;
Beneath their boughs the shadows dwell,
  And shed a soft delicious gloom.

All else is bathed in living light,
  That thrills the soul with joy intense—
Alas! that falling dews of night
  Must warn a convalescent hence.

Stevens Point, 28 May 1871
Milwaukee Daily Sentinel, 3 June 1871

BLUE GENTIANS.

The prairies are fair in their summer array—
June roses are lovely, and asters are gay;
Yet there is not a flower that can speak to the heart,
Like the gentian, that blooms when the others depart.

We feel, as we gaze on its delicate fringe,
Its clustering grace, its ethereal tinge,
(No sky ever smiled more enchantingly blue,)
That Summer's last flower is her loveliest, too.

So blooming and bright, in the midst of decay,
So cheerful when sunlight is passing away,
Its radiant beauty seems born of the sky,
To bid us look upward when sorrow is nigh.

Milwaukee Daily Sentinel, 8 November 1870

ONCE MORE.

Once more I stand among the hills,
  Once more the mountains meet my gaze,
While solemn awe my spirit thrills,
  As in the well-remembered days
When yonder village was my home,
  And all the world beyond, to me,
  Was one wide realm of mystery,
Whose paths I longed, yet feared, to roam.

I smile in thinking of the fears
  That shadowed o'er my spirit then.
I would not ask to live the years
  Of youth and childhood o'er again;
A happier home is mine to-day—
  Beyond the prairies of the West,
  A broader faith, a calmer rest,
Albeit my locks are tinged with gray.

The mountains have for me a voice
  I knew not in those days of yore;
Listening, I hear it, and rejoice—
  "God is our Father evermore."
Not only of the chosen few
  That safe in sheltered valleys dwell,
  But of the vaster host as well,
That from the loftiest height we view.

The more I tread the paths of life,
  And mingle with the multitude,
The more—in spite of sin and strife—
  I know and feel that God is good;
And that upon the heavenly plains,
  Full many a ransomed soul shall stand,
  To whom we would not reach a hand
To lift them from earth's mire and stains.

Our Father, in this presence vast,
  Among these everlasting hills,
I fain would make an holocaust

Of all my selfish aims and wills.
Oh! may my spirit be imbued
    With grace and charity divine;
    To know *Thy* friends, and make them mine,
Among earth's busy multitude.

Brownington, Vermont, 20 July 1872
Milwaukee Daily Sentinel, 10 August 1872

GEORGE REED.
THE PROJECTOR AND BUILDER OF THE WISCONSIN CEN-TRAL RAILWAY.[45]

[Accompanying the Presentation of a Watch.]

Long years in solitude we dwelt,
  From busy, bustling life apart;
The world's great pulse we scarcely felt,
  Or heard the beating of its heart.

And if at times some restless wight
  Aspired to glance at life without,
How wearily, from morn till night,
  The stage-coach bore him on his route.

Behold the change! Some magic wand
  Has brought the railroad to our door;
We clasp the world's extended hand,
  And feel a thrill unfelt before.

We come to-night with grateful hearts,
  To know what kind enchanter's *reed*
Has vanquished all opposing arts,
  And "brought this happy chance to speed."[46]

Like iron that his workmen weld,
  His brave, indomitable will
Its chosen purpose firmly held,
  Unchanged, "through good report and ill."[47]

Though countless obstacles arose,
  His patient courage faced them down,
And, now his work draws near its close,
  He well deserves a laurel crown.

In stead, we bring an offering slight,
  Whose quiet utterance may express,
At every hour of day or night,
  How thankfully his name we bless.

January 1874

[45] "Lines by Ada J. Moore, read by Mr. Clarkson at Menasha, Jan. 9, 1874."

[46] A line from Walter Scott's *Lady of the Lake,* Canto 6 (1810).

[47] Sir Walter Scott in *The Field of Waterloo* (1815).

SONGS OF THE WAR

WHAT SHALL THE END BE?

What shall the end be?
    Brethren are at strife—
The children of one mother
Shout, in their deadly hatred of each other,
    "War! to the knife!"

Let sterner hearts exult,
    That the dark tides of war
Will o'er our country sweep;
I am a woman, and I can but weep
    That such things are.

In this most anxious hour,
    I think, with starting tears,
Of one—a maiden fair—
Who used the sorrows and the joys to share
    Of my young years.

Her home was near my own,
    And we were oft together,
Whiling away the hours
In gathering by the brook the early flowers,
    In sunny weather.

Widely diverging paths
    Our feet since then have trod;
Here, in the free Northwest,
Is my heart-home, and here my children rest—
    Beneath the sod.

She for the "Sunny South,"
    Her mountain home forsook,
And rules a servile band
Of toiling slaves, they say, with a haughty hand,
    And queenly look.

'T is sad to think that she,
    The friend of my young life,
Should be, in heart and hand,

Linked with the foes and traitors of our land,
    In this dark strife.

    Yet there's a sadder thought:
      Not friendship's bonds alone
Are crumbled into dust;
But *Nature's* ties, the holiest and the first,
    Are trampled on.

    What shall the end be?
      Who, but God, can tell?
In this terrific hour,
There is no hope but in Almighty power,
    The storm to quell.

Wisconsin State Rights, 7 May 1861

"God is in history." Not alone the Past
This signet wears, eternally to last;
The painful Present, with its shadowing cloud,
The dreaded Future darker mists enshroud,
Shall, when these clouds are rolled away, reveal
The same inscription, as with pen of steel,
Traced, it may be, in characters of blood,
Yet traced indelibly—*the name of God.*

When first our nation struggled into birth,
While tempests raged whose throes convulsed the earth,
Yet Freedom's star shone on serenely fair,
A world exclaimed. "The hand of God is there!"
In later days, when clouds have gathered round,
And muttering thunder rolled along the ground,
Still has that star maintained her glorious sway,
Save one dark blot, with undiminished ray.

But now, we deem, has dawned a darker hour—
The earthquake threatens, while the tempests lower,
And fearful omens throng upon the sight,
That all our hopes shall sink in endless night.
Not so! By all the glories of the Past!
God is in History still! These skies o'ercast
Shall smile again beneath the cloudless ray
Of Freedom's star, *her one blot wiped away!*

Milwaukee Daily Sentinel, 7 February 1861

Traitor! I read thy name,[48]
  Once, with a glow of pride;
But now my cheek with deepest flush of shame,
  For thee, false heart, is dyed.

Alas! who could have thought,
  That from the lofty place
Whereon thou stoodst in the high realms of thought,
  Thou thus couldst woo disgrace?

Not from thy favorite sea
  Didst thou this treachery learn;
The waves that seem but fitting types of thee,
  True to their tides return.

And even the storms obey
  The fixed and changeless laws
Of Him who sent them on their destined way—
  The great eternal Cause.

But thou, untaught by these,
  Hast trampled in the dust
Thy country's laws, and made her liberties
  An offering to thy lust—

The greedy lust of power;
  Yet, ingrate, on thy head
Honor and wealth, in many a lavish shower,
  Thy country's hand hath shed.

Henceforth awaits for thee
  The traitor's darkest doom;
Thine injured country's latest gift shall be
  Dishonor in the tomb.

---

[48] Matthew Fontaine Maury (1806-1873) was a naval officer and pioneer in the study of oceanography who joined the Confederacy at the outbreak of the Civil War. The poem was also published in the *Wisconsin State Rights,* 5 June 1861, with the headnote: "The following was sent to and published in the Milwaukee *Sentinel,* but was so shockingly mutilated, we publish it in a corrected form.—*Ed. State Rights.*"

The star that rose on high,
  And heralded thy fame,
Is blotted out forever from our sky,
  By thy dark deed of shame.

Milwaukee Daily Sentinel, 24 May 1861

THE WOUNDED SOLDIER GATHERING VIOLETS.

The soldier-boy lay in the forest shade,
  With a mossy bank for his pillow,
And a slumberous sound the breezes made,
  And they swayed the oak and the willow.

Weary with battle-strife, fainting with heat,
  And worn with the long day's marching,
Yet vainly he longed for a slumber sweet,
  Beneath the cool shade over-arching.

From a wound half hid in his dark brown hair,
  The life-drops were ceaselessly flowing,
And the pain seemed more than the boy could bear—
  From the flush on his young cheek glowing.

But his yearning eyes that had been upturned
  To the sky with a touching sadness,
As they fell to earth, in a moment burned
  With a yet more touching gladness.

Wood-violets—blue as the sky above—
  Were clustering closely around him,
And it seemed to the boy that a breath of love
  From his mountain home had found him.

He gathered the flowers within his reach,
  Then, painfully turning over,
Sought more—to his parched lips pressing each,
  With the eagerness of a lover.

Help came at last, and they bore him away—
  His violets still caressing,
With a smile that said, more than words could say,
  Of tender and grateful blessing.

Stevens Point, 20 May 1864
Milwaukee Sentinel, 11 June 1864
Wisconsin Lumberman, 3 August 1864

THE DEFEAT OF OUR ARMIES.
[After Bull Run.][49]

'T is a dark hour—to Heaven we lift our eyes,
  In deep and voiceless woe;
A thunderbolt has fallen from the skies
  When least we feared the blow.
Because our armies trusted not in God,
  But in their own right hand,
Our pride hath felt at length His chastening rod,
  And darkness fills our land.

There hath gone up to Heaven a wail of anguish
  From myriad homes to day,
Blent with the cries and groans of those who languish
  In pain their lives away.
God helps the hearts that mourn, and bring the dying
  To that eternal home,
Where wars no more shall be, and groans and sighing
  And death shall never come.

Yet, let us not sink tamely in the dust,
  And yield our righteous cause,
But in the "God of Battles" put our trust,
  And reverence His laws.
Then will He lead our armies to the field,
  As in the former days,
And when to Freedom, Tyranny shall yield,
  To Him be all the praise.

Milwaukee Daily Sentinel, 1 August 1861

---

[49] Appeared with the headnote: "The following neat little sonnet comes to us from our gifted contributor, Ada J. Moore. It breathes the true spirit of devotion and patriotism joined."

THE FOURTH OF JULY, 1863.

Thank God for thee, illustrious day—[50]
  Baptized anew with glory;
Long after we have passed away,
  Our sons shall tell thy story.

Shall tell how haughty Vicksburg fell,
  Before whose walls stupendous,
In days gone by our soldiery
  Met slaughter so tremendous.

How Lee's invading chivalry—
  Their daring schemes defeated,
Before the hosts of Liberty
  Ingloriously retreated.

City and hamlet ring to-night
  With shouts and joyful voices;
Midst cannon peal and blaze of light,
  Each patriot heart rejoices.

Thank God! No other words than these
  Can give our thoughts expression;
A nation on its bended knees
  Thanks God for its salvation.

Milwaukee Daily Sentinel, 25 July 1863

---

[50] The day that marked Union victories at Vicksburg and Gettysburg.

SEED-TIME AND HARVEST.

The seed-time comes—the spring-time fair,
A flood of sunlight warms the air.

Along the wayside—faintly seen—
Appears a delicate tinge of green.

The music of the April showers
Wakens to life the slumbering flowers.

The robin, on the leafless tree,
Sees tiny buds expand, with glee,

And pours his soul out in a lay,
As sweetly changeful as the day.

The farmer o'er the brown bare plain,
Scatters broadcast his choicest grain.

With thoughtful brow, he wonders whether
The welcome rains and sunny weather

Will bless him with abundant crops.
Or frost and tempest blight his hopes.

I, too, in thinking of a plain—
Thick-sown, alas, with richer grain—

The plain of Gettysburg, must ponder
The self-same thought, with deeper wonder.

This lavished grain of blood and tears,
What will it yield in future years?

A harvest worthy to be sung?
Worthy the seed from whence it sprung?

Or will the blight of party strife—
With fraud and base corruption rife—

The patriot's highest hopes defeat,
And render victory incomplete?

We can but hope, we can but trust—
We know our God is wise and just,

And still his promise must prevail—
"Seed-time and Harvest shall not fail."[51]

Milwaukee Daily Sentinel, 25 April 1864

---

[51] Genesis 8:22: God's promise to Noah not to destroy the earth by flood again.

THOUGHTS AT A PIC-NIC.

A brilliant day, a sunny sky,
A mirthful group of friends near by—
Yet scarcely can I bear to stay
Where smiles are bright and words are gay.

The stately oaks above my head
Their welcome canopy have spread;
The wild-wood flowers around me spring,
And humming bees are on the wing.

Yet, as I listen to the chimes
Of nature's sweet "unwritten rhymes,"
Blent with the ringing laughter-peals,
No sense of gladness o'er me steals.

I close my eyes and see instead
A field of battle, gory-red,
Where serried hosts, with banners flying,
Rush onward, o'er the dead and dying.

Instead of nature's peaceful tones,
I hear the wounded soldier's moans,
And death-shrieks louder than the peal
Of drum and fife and clashing steel.

I see them, true, as in a dream—
The charging hosts, the bayonet's gleam,
Yet may not Richmond's field of blood,
Ere this have made the vision good?

When anxious nations listening wait
The tidings of our country's fate,
Whose welfare, and perchance whose life,
Hangs on the issue of the strife—

When wives and daughters wait in fear
The news they scarce can brook to hear—
When mothers weep beside the hearth—
God knows, *these hours are not for mirth.*

Milwaukee Daily Sentinel, 20 August 1862

Lift the standard! true hearts, rally,
  Once again around the flag!
With no traitor pause to dally,
  Let no faltering footstep lag.

Onward! With the hearts of men,
  Men who know not how to yield;
Strive with heart and voice and pen,
  O'er our wide-spread battle-field.

Plant our flag on every corner,
  Let all hearts yield homage to it;
If there pass an open scorner,
  May some strong arm bid him rue it!

There's no time for dallying now—
  Every man must know his post,
If we seek to overthrow
  Treason's base opposing host.

With our armies, bravely fighting,
  That our country may be free,
Let us, heart and hand uniting,
  Win a two-fold victory.

Then shall God's fair angel, Peace.
  Lift her smiling, stainless face,
And the mourners' tears shall cease,
  Midst a nation's songs of praise.

Milwaukee Daily Sentinel, 5 October 1864 as "A Rallying Cry"

Wisconsin to Missouri—
Free Missouri,
Sendeth greeting,
Blessings sendeth,
Proudly her right hand extendeth;
Every heart, with pleasure beating,
Welcomes thee,
From the curse of slavery free.[52]
Hail! with thine enfranchised sister,
Maryland, "our Maryland!"
Ye have burst your bonds asunder,
Flung the galling yoke from off ye—
Though the nations gaze in wonder,
Not a voice is raised to scoff ye;
All in reverence stand,
Owning the mighty Hand
That out of darkness brings forth light,
O'er war's visage dark and gory
Shedding affluence of glory,
Better than the smile of peace.
Not in vain God's hand hath tried thee,
Not in vain thy fierce baptism—
Blood and fire have purified thee,
Made thee meet for Freedom's chrism—
Holier far than Rome's.
When this conflict dire shall cease,
And the day-star shall arise
Whose first dawning greets our eyes,
O'er all thy peaceful homes
The smile of God shall rest,
And thy fertile soil,
'Neath the freeman's toil,
Shall make thee the pride of our glorious West.
Then once again, all hail!
Missouri, the free!

---

[52] Missouri, which had not been included in the 1863 Emancipation Proclamation, abolished slavery on 11 January 1865. Maryland had passed a similar law on 1 November 1864.

Let the joyful shout from all hearts ring out—
    "We welcome thee!"

15 January 1865

Milwaukee Daily Sentinel, 21 January 1865 as "A Song of Welcome"

The war is ended—God be praised!
  Our boys are marching home;
With blood-stained banners proudly raised,
  And triumph-songs, they come.

We welcome them with open arms,
  With hearts that throb and yearn;
To home and love, with all their charms,
  We hail their safe return.

Our country, through the coming years,
  Shall honor, gratefully,
These war-worn men, her royal peers,
  Her true nobility.

Yet those who close beside them stood,
  With hearts as true and brave,
Who shed as lavishly their blood,
  The nation's life to save,—

Who, though the hue of night they wore,
  No deeds of darkness wrought;
Whose faithful hands our banner bore,
  From many a field well fought;

Whose heart one cheering hope sustained—
  That, for their blood outpoured,
The rights of freemen, nobly gained,
  Should be their rich reward;

For them, no shouts of welcome rise,
  No plaudits rend the sky;
Theirs is the toil and sacrifice,
  But not the victory.

The hand that laid the bayonet down,
  The ballot may not claim;
Theirs is the cross, and ours the crown—
  Enfranchised but in name.

Yet, courage! Freedmen of the Lord!
  The Hand that broke your chains
Shall yet bestow the full reward
  Of all your toil and pains.

Stevens Point, 6 June 1865
Milwaukee Daily Sentinel, 16 June 1865

EARLY POEMS

SUMMER DAYS.

By Ada I. Moore

Morn—and the flow'rets wake
  From their dewy rest,
And joyous ripples break
  O'er the lakelet's breast;
And the birds and the breeze
Are like harps in the trees,
  By angel hands prest.

Noon—and the cattle stand
  In the cooling shade;
O'er the dry and dusty land
  The flowerets fade;
And the faint zephyrs fly
From the parched sultry sky,
  To the forest glade.

Night—and the sun has set,
  Erewhile, in the west;
On high the stars are met,
  In their glory drest.
With the birds and the flowers,
In the night-shaded bowers,
  Let us seek our rest.

Castle Hill, Vermont, 27 August 1851
Orleans County Gazette, 2 October 1851[53]

---

[53] Reprinted in *Wisconsin Pinery,* 12 July 1855, and dated "Pine Cottage, July 9th, 1855."

THE CRY OF THE HEATHEN.

By Jessie Moore

Ocean, in thy peerless glory,
   Proudly dashing on our shore,
Whence the sad and mournful story
   Borne thy foaming billows o'er?
Breezes, o'er the waters winging,
   Wandered from the Eastern sky,
Whence the echoes ye are bringing,
   "Give us teachers, or we die!"

'T is from Afric's distant plains,
   Long by darkest crime defiled—
From the Sultan's wide domains,
   From the Kurdish mountains wild—
Lo! Armenia's harvest fair,
   Ready for the sickle stands,
Perishing for want of care,
   Yet how few the reaper-bands!

Christians, rouse ye from your slumbers!
   View the heathen world awake;
Lo! To vast and eager numbers,
   You the bread of life may break.
From the hamlets of the mountains,
   Hear the Macedonian cry[54]—
"Lead us to the healing fountains,
   Come and help us, or we die."

'T is on *you* for aid they call—
   Will ye coldly slumber on?
Waken, ere the heathen fall—
   Bid the Gospel on them dawn;
Yield yourselves, your wealth, your time,
   Nor to sinful sloth give way,
Till o'er earth's remotest clime,
   Spreads the glad millennial day.

Vermont Chronicle, 21 October 1851

---

[54] Allusion to Acts 16:9-10.

Help, Lord, the godly ceaseth!
  On earth the faithful fail;
Well may our stricken spirits
  Take up the mourner's wail.
A man of God hath fallen,[55]
  A Champion of the Cross,
Whose noble spirit counted
  All else on earth but dross.

Where flows the broad Missouri,
  They laid him down to rest,
And flowers that gem the prairie,
  Shall bloom above his breast.
Yet 'mid our verdant mountains
  Full many a heart hath bled,
In sacred tears embalming
  The memory of the dead.

Awhile he moved among us—
  These hills and valleys trod,
Until it seemed an angel
  Was sent to bless the sod.
His message was Salvation,
  His theme, Redeeming Love,
And oh! his melting accents
  A heart of stone might move.

That form and mien majestic,
  Our hearts can ne'er forget—
Those eyes with ardor beaming,
  Or with compassion wet;
Still in our memory dwelleth
  The deep impassioned voice,
That in a Savior's mercy
  Bade our sad hearts rejoice.

---

[55] Rev. James Gallagher (1792-1853), prominent Presbyterian minister from Tennessee who died in Missouri. Chaplain of the U. S. House of Representatives from 1852-1853.

But he has passed before us,
  To mansions of the blest—
Oh! may his sacred mantle
  Upon our spirits rest.
May we with holy ardor
  Pursue the path *he* trod,
And hope in bliss to meet him,
  When summoned home to God.

Vermont Chronicle, 29 November 1853

TWILIGHT FANCIES.

Oh, there are times when thoughts of life,
With all its strange mysterious strife
Of hope and fear, of good and ill,
Of dark despair and dauntless will—
Where'er a human heart doth beat,
Or flowers are crushed by human feet—
From sky to sky, from pole to pole—
Do strangely overwhelm the soul.

'T was thus this eve, in pensive mood,
Apart in listlessness I stood,
Watching the last bright beam of day
In gold and crimson melt away,
And yielding to the mystic power,
The holy spell of Twilight's hour—
When o'er the spirit steals a sense
Of some unearthly influence.

And as amid that silent dream
Of things that are and things that seem,
Rose sad repining thoughts of life,
With all its sorrow, sin and strife—
A vision o'er my fancy stole—
A panorama of the soul—
The soul of man, that none may know,
Jehovah's breath, Jehovah's foe.

That vision fair yet strange to view,
I ween an angel's pencil drew,
And from its light my spirit caught
A realm of new and grateful thought.
The world is dull and cold of mien—
It shall not know what I have seen;
It scoffs at Faith, and sneers at Art,
But shall not mock a dreamer's heart.

Orleans County Gazette, 11 September 1852,
Wisconsin Pinery, 10 June 1857 as "Lines"

THE CONTRAST.

I.

Sitting, at the close of day,
  By my window, gloomily,
To consuming care a prey,
  Time was passing wearily.
Life was sad and dark and drear—
Not a sight or sound of cheer—
Friends were far and foes were near—
  Joy was but a mockery.

In those early days of youth
  Life was dark with agony,
And the beacon-light of truth
  Shone not on its mystery.
Then I learned the cruel art,
In my wounded, bleeding heart
Deeper yet to crush the dart,
  And to love my misery.

II.

Musing at the close of day,
  By my window pleasantly,
Driving gloomy care away—
  Hours are flitting cheerily.
Life has many a sunny spot—
Friendship smiles upon my lot,[56]
And in castle or in cot,
  Bounds my spirit merrily.

In these later days of youth,
  Life is still a mystery;
But the heavenly light of Truth
  Gilds the darkness cheeringly.
I have learned the wiser art—
From the wounded, bleeding heart
To withdraw the poisoned dart—
  Shunning selfish misery.[57]

Milwaukee Daily Sentinel, 6 February 1861 as "Now and Then"
Wisconsin State Journal, 24 March 1865 as "A Contrast"

---

[56] In 1861, the last three lines of this stanza read, "Love and friendship bless my lot— / Though my griefs are not forgot, / Still my heart swells gratefully."

[57] A version of the last four lines of this stanza is excerpted in the *Wood County Reporter*, 5 January 1893, in a collection of "Excellent Quotations" and attributed to Ada J. Moore—"Strive to learn the blessed art / To withdraw the poisoned dart / Ere it reaches to the heart / Shunning selfish misery."

She came as cometh a summer cloud
  In the azure deep of heaven;
And we gazed on her infant beauty, proud
  Of the treasure God had given.

She was like a cloud—such a gentle grace
  With each motion seemed to blend,
As follows them when in azure space
  Their fairy-like forms extend.

Her brow like the snowy cloud-wreath seemed,
  That floats on the evening gale,
And her eyes in their angel-beauty gleamed
  Like stars from their curtaining veil.

She came as cometh a summer cloud—
  In a gentle morn of May;
But oh! she lies in a snow-white shroud—
  Like a cloud hath she passed away.

Pine Cottage, March 1855 [58]
Wisconsin Pinery, 15 March 1855 as "Maria"
Milwaukee Daily Sentinel, 12 January 1861 as "Our Wee One"

---

[58] Given the date when this first appeared, it is unlikely she originally wrote this about one of her own children. It might have been written for a relative or friend. She did later use it as the obituary poem for Mary Ada Phillips, d. 18 August 1858 (*Wisconsin Pinery,* 10 September 1858).

I sought a theme, and cast an earnest eye
O'er nature's scenes, perchance to find it there.
Night's azure sky was o'er me, gemmed with stars—
Those mystic orbs that "teach as well as shine";[59]
Around me fell the moonbeams, like a charm
Holding the earth entranced, so hushed and still
Was that fair landscape in its robe of light.
Then spoke the false and siren voice of Fame:
"Write not of *these;* too oft have harps been strung
To nature's ceaseless praises, for the scene
That thrills thy spirit now, is not more fair
Than woke the raptures of the Mantuan bard,
Or Sappho witnessed from the Lesbian hills.
Seek yet another theme."
                  So then I turned
To the wide world of Art, and there I saw
Life mocked in marble, paintings half divine,
Wondrous inventions, all the elements—
Whose single rage might wreck a universe—
Made man's obedient servants; and I gazed
In admiration.
                But the Siren said,
"Write not of these—more lofty be thy theme,
So may thy words an answering echo wake
In gifted hearts."
                Then did I raise my eyes,
The *finite* scorned, to seek the *Infinite;*
It was but *One*—yet One in Trinity—
Vast—mighty—deep—incomprehensible—
Sure—uncreated—self-existent ever,
Creating mind eternal as Itself,
In all perfections infinite—in power
Not unsurpassed by wisdom, crowned with love.
I stood bewildered in the rash attempt
To fathom Deity, when a still small voice
Breathed in my ear, I knew not whence or how,

---

[59] Edward Young (1745), *The Complaint; Or, Night Thoughts,* Night Ninth, The Consolation, line 636.

"Shall finite measure Infinite, or comprehend?
Vain mortal, *look into thy heart and write!*[60]
Humbled, I turned me from the outer world
To the neglected portals of my breast,
And wandered through its chambers.
                                   Scarce I dreamed
To meet such strange assemblage. There were thoughts
I knew not that I cherished—hopes and fears,
Passions and prejudices, lights and shades—
Blent in strange harmony. Affections there
Were basking in the sunny light of love;
But some were wounded—words and looks are darts
Oft tipped with keenest poison—and they sate
With drooping eyes apart, and wept their wrongs.
Some clung to earth, its honors, joys and friends,
Read nature's book of loveliness, or sought
To twine their brows with Science's glittering gems.
And some—alas! how few!—had raised their eyes
From sin and sorrow, and delusive joys,
To look upon the Sufferer of the Cross,
And fixed their hopes in Heaven. Thus I roamed
Through the strange castle of the human mind,
And thought how wise the ancient precept given
To one who sought for wisdom—*Know thyself.*
I felt how little I had known my heart,
Or dreamed of Passion's Etna slumbering there,
Or the wild thoughts that ever come and go
As flies the shaft of Heaven—yet leave a trace,
A *darkened* trace, to mark their baleful course.
And oh! I felt that naught but power divine,
From sin with all its train of bitter woe,
Can keep the heart—*the erring heart of man.*

---

[60] The phrase in italics is from Phillip Sidney, *Astrophil and Stella,* Sonnet 1 (1591).

My father, do I dream,
Or have the suns of three-score weary years,
With all their joys and sorrows, hopes and fears,
  Shone on thy path with many a changeful gleam.

What varied scenes must rise
In Memory's picture-galleries of the Past,
Radiant with light, or darkly overcast
  With clouds that shadow life's inconstant skies.

What memories of the dead,
The friends and playmates that thy childhood knew,
Companions of thy youth, the fond and true,
  Who long have slumbered in a dreamless bed.

And, dearer far than these,
The loved ones from thy fond embraces riven,
Whose smiles once made thy home an earthly heaven,
  And woke thy spirit's tenderest sympathies.

And do no fond thoughts arise
Within thy heart, of those who widely roam
From early friends and childhood's cherished home,
  Who think of thee to-night with tearful eyes?

Life hath been long to thee—
Not as men reckon seasons on the earth,
But long in all that gives to life its worth—
  In faith and hope, in zeal and charity.

And still thou toilest on,
While calmly waiting for that solemn day
When earth and earthly scenes shall pass away,
  And all thy cares and joys and griefs be done.

Far distant be that hour!
Long may'st thou dwell in calm and tranquil rest
Amidst the hearts thy love hath ever blessed—
  A dearer treasure than earth's richest dower.

Pine Cottage, 27 October 1855
Wisconsin Pinery, 26 November 1855

MIDNIGHT MUSINGS.

Out in the silent night-air let me go,
    And list the autumn breeze
Come laden with its lonely tones of woe,
    Among the leafless trees.

'T is wild, and desolate, and dreary, all—
    Low sweep the trailing clouds,
And starless, cheerless darkness, like a pall,
    The gloomy scene enshrouds.

And yet my spirit feels a strange delight,
    Alone to linger here—
To list the wailing "voices of the night,"
    That fall on Fancy's ear.

With a mysterious sympathy endued,
    And made by suffering bold,
Converse with Nature, in her darkest mood
    My spirit yearns to hold.

But the false breeze has chilled me to the heart;
    Damp, noxious vapors rise,
And warn me the dark influence to depart
    Of midnight's baleful skies.

Father of Love! to thee I turn. Forgive
    Each impulse rash and wild;
For duty and for thee henceforth to live,
    Assist thine erring child.

Milwaukee Daily Sentinel, 14 March 1861 as "Musings"

"Wanted—an angel, for Heaven!"
  And the soft air felt the sweep
Of a strong and rushing pinion,
  Through the far cerulean deep.
But the seraph's wings were folded,
  As he stood on the dewy earth,
When the holy hush of Twilight
  Was stilling its sounds of mirth.

One moment brief he lingered,
  For the scene was strangely fair,
'Neath the soft and dreamy radiance
  Of the star-lit evening air.
"The soul must sigh at parting,"
  Spake the visitant unseen,
"But the bowers of Heaven are brighter,
  In their fresh and fadeless green."

A gentle child was lisping
  Its low-voiced evening prayer—
Nor dreamed that a viewless watcher
  Stood smiling on him there.
But hushed were the tones of music,
  And drooped the fair young head,
As up to the gates of Heaven
  Two bright-winged angels sped.

Pine Cottage, January 1855
Wisconsin Pinery, 12 February 1855 as "The Child Angel"

CORA.
A TEMPERANCE SKETCH.

She stood beside the altar. Her slight form
Was fittingly attired in purest white,
And midst her tresses, whose resplendent hue
Might shame a raven's plumage, one sweet rose
Had nestled lovingly. Upon her brow—
Her gentle brow as alabaster fair—
Sat woman's firm, confiding, constant trust,
With girlhood's timid fearfulness combined.
On her transparent cheek the glowing hue
That came and went as clouds on summer sky,
Bespoke the varied feelings of her heart.
But oh! her eyes—what pencil can portray
Th' expression of those "windows of the soul"?
The lustrous orbs, that in retiring grace
Were wont to smile beneath the dewy lids
That graceful drooped above them, now lit up
With deep emotion and conflicting thought,
Spoke at each glance what words could not express—
Volumes of tenderness, as erst they fell
Upon the manly being at her side—
Her first and best beloved.
                 His form was cast
In nature's proudest mould—his countenance bore
The impress of a high and lofty soul—
Nor bore it falsely; from his eagle eye
Gleamed all a poet's fire, and fervor wild,
And his whole frame seemed but one pulse of bliss,
As on his soul he took the solemn vow
To cherish well the loved one at his side,
While life and strength remained.
                     With her's his soul
Was tuned in unison—her favorites, his—
The flowers he loved she trained with tenderest care—
Each lived but for the other.
                    Time passed on,
And still beheld them happy. Fortune smiled,
Fame lured him onward with her meteor glare,
Yet in their peaceful home content was found,

And pure domestic bliss, so rare on earth.
The anniversary of their bridal morn
Once and again returned; but ere the third,
A tiny cloud stole o'er their smiling sky—
Unfeared at first, so harmless did it seem,
Attired in pleasing form to win the eye—
But soon its folds increased and darker grew.
Quickly her watchful eye of faithful love
Beheld the gathering storm, and vainly strove
To check its progress, but alas! too late!
Slowly but surely came the tempest on,
And spent its wrath on their devoted heads.

   *   *   *   *   *   *   *   *

Five fleeting years are passed—again the sun
Brings the return of that auspicious day
That rang their wedding peal. Within the church
Where their young lips pronounced the holy vows,
A sad procession enters. On the bier
A coffin slow is borne, and following close
Behold a fragile form with faltering step.
'T is she—that maiden fair—but oh! how changed!
Her countenance bears the impress of a grief
No power of man can soothe. Her cheek is pale,
And as the funeral knell its solemn note
Rings mournful on the ear, she breathes a sigh
Laden with untold bitterness of woe.
The pure white drapery that decked her then,
Has given place to robes of darkest hue;
But from her face she lifts the sombre veil,
To look upon the bier.
                   Approach and gaze!
Behold whose form in death reposes there,
And learn her cause of grief!
                     Nay! start not back!
Although the sight be loathsome and repulsive.
That bloated form, five little years ago,
"Th' observed of all observers," charmed each eye
With easy winning grace and noble mien,
As at her side he stood who weepeth now

In deep heart-broken anguish o'er his bier.
Oh, say what power of earth or hell could change
That manly form of noble intellect—
Jehovah's image—to a wretch like this?
Oh! breathe it not aloud, lest hell rejoice,
And angels weep and shudder at the sound—
That foe to God and man, *the monster* RUM!
Hath set his seal debasing on that brow.
Why, why must it thus be, that power is given
To *fiends* on earth—I will not call them men,
To change the grain that smiling o'er the fields,
Invites the reaper's hand, and food might give
To thousand starving creatures of the earth,
Into a maddening, brain-destroying thing—
Transforming what the great Jehovah made
Scarce lower than the angels, to a brute?
And shall we lay our hands upon our lips,
And calmly gaze upon a scene like this,
Scarce even hoping that the time will come
When they shall be no more?
     Or shall we go,
With softly whispered words and honeyed mien,
And ask the shameless authors of the ruin
To cease this murderous traffic? Do we dream,
While they remorseless act a part like this,
That "Moral Suasion" will their hand restrain?
Ah! rest no longer in such vain belief!
Let not the laws which ye have helped to make
Be trampled thus upon, and laughed to scorn.
Wake! Wake! Remove the dens of sin and crime,
That pour their frightful streams of liquid fire
O'er our blest happy land, and with the Pledge,
The blessed Pledge of Total Abstinence,
Within the hands, and kind words on thy lips—
Go quickly forth, and save thy fellow man,
While yet thou canst, from such a fearful doom,
And God be with thee in thy work of love.

APPENDIX:
MISCELLANEOUS NEWSPAPER ITEMS

TOUTE SEULE.
[ALONE]

By Esperanza

Priex pour moi,
Car, lorequo vient le nult
Je penou a toi—
Helas! Toute seule je suis.

Priex pour moi—
A notre Fere aux cleux,
Car, moi, je erole
Qu'est n'est moins père que Dieu.

Priex pour moi,
Ta vie aut boune et pure;
Bouhour pour toi!
Ma vie est triste et dure.

Priex pour moi;
Je suis a mes genoux—
Je prie pour toi,
Je prie—et que fais tu?

Milwaukee Daily Sentinel, 16 March 1865

A Wisconsin Poetess. [61]

UNDER THE PINES. By Ada J. Moore
West & Co., Milwaukee, Wis.

Ada J. Moore is a name not unfamiliar to Wisconsin readers. It has been the privilege to publish a number of her contributions, and they have attracted great attention and elicited unqualified praise. Her's is an exquisitely poetic temperament, and it is not extravagant to say that she writes because she cannot help it. When she puts upon the title page of this, her first volume, the lines of Mrs. Browning,

> "The world is weak,
> And what we best conceive, we fail to speak,"

she is more modest than just. In fact, her power of expression equals the beauty of her conceptions, and she shows a complete and accurate mastery over a varied and effective rhythm. We can find space for only a single poem, though we make the selection with diffidence, and do not assume that it is fairly representative of her best work. . . . [see *SEED-TIME AND HARVEST*, above]

We believe that the volume before us will be recognized as a handsome product of the printers' and binders' art, and take pleasure in stating that it is the work of The Sentinel job-office and bindery.

Milwaukee Daily Sentinel, 24 December 1874

---

[61] The headline for the "Literary" column is "A Volume of Poems by a Talented Wisconsin Poetess."

Under the Pines.

This new volume of poems by Ada J. Moore, is meeting with a rapid sale in this city, where the gifted authoress is so well and favorably known. And well it may, for the book has merits far beyond and above any local interest that its publication may have excited. It contains gems in poetry that must give the writer a fame as great as her fondest ambition ever dared to hope for. With her the muses seem to be ever present, and therefore the style of the book is not labored, but easy and graceful, from beginning to end. . . .

Stevens Point Daily Journal, 2 January 1875

Book Notices.

UNDER THE PINES. By Ada J. Moore.
> When I attain to utter forth in verse
> Some inward thought, my soul throbs audibly
> Along my pulses, yearning to be free.
> > The world is weak.
> And what we best conceive, we fail to speak.
> > *—Mrs. Browning.*

West & Co.: Milwaukee, 1875.

A friend of the author, whose literary taste will not be questioned, placed this volume of Mrs. Moore's poems on our table with the remark that it contained poems of great merit.

Mrs. Moore resides at Stevens Point, we believe, and it is "Under the Pines" of that romantic region that she writes. She has been blessed with thirteen children. Tennyson could not say of her half scornfully, that "a brace of twins will weed her of her folly."[62] She has suffered and grown strong. When she writes of love and of little ones passed away we know that her words come from the depths of a mother's heart. It is genuine joy or real anguish that moves her. For the benefit of those who are single and to show the cheerfulness and courage of a mother in Israel, and a poet, we quote the last two verses from her "Plea for Matrimony."

We have room for one gem from these bright pages, entitled, "Through the Pines."

It is not often that we find a little love story so happily told as this. Only a poet could do it with so much delicacy and grace.

Wisconsin State Journal, 17 December 1875

---

[62] The quotation is from Alfred, Lord Tennyson's *The Princess*, canto 5, lines 453-54 (1850).

A Poetess Reviews a Poetess.

UNDER THE PINES. By Ada J. Moore. West & Co., Milwaukee, Wis.
[To the Editor of the Milwaukee Sentinel.]

We have been spending an hour "Under the Pines," this evening, and instead of beating the wailing winds, and shivering in the wintry blasts, we seemed to bask in the sunlight of love, and listen to the strains of sweet music, struck from the lyre of Poesy.

"Under the Pines," is the pretty title of a new volume of poems, by one of Wisconsin's gifted women, "Ada J. Moore." The volume contains over 200 pages, and is tastily printed on tinted paper, and is essentially a book for the home circle and the fireside. The book breathes and burns with the fire of motherly and wifely devotion, and in this line the author has made her happiest hits, and shows her finest powers.

By far the finest poem in the volume, according to our ideas, is one entitled "To my Husband," . . .

The poem is exquisite throughout, breathing the perfection of wifely devotion in every sounded verse. "Naming the Baby," "Nellie," "After the Rain," "A Plea for Matrimony," "A Wish Unwished," "My Lost Jewels," "La Petite," all throb with the heart of the wife and mother, and are among the best poems the volume contains.

The patriot, also, breathes in some of the poems—written during the war—and the whole volume bespeaks for the author a love of the right, and true, and a desire to lift the burden of the oppressed, and help the suffering ones of earth, rather than an ambition for literary distinction. "Under the Pines," will repay perusal, and is a credit to its author and to Wisconsin—the state which contributes more to Eastern literature than all other Western states combined.

E. W.[63]

This book is now on sale at our various book stores. It would make a very appropriate Christmas present.

Stevens Point Daily Journal, 18 December 1875

---

[63] "E. W." is likely the poet Ella Wheeler (Wilcox), who published numerous poems in the *Milwaukee Daily Sentinel* in the 1870s.

The Cheapest Christmas Gift in Town,
A $1.50 Book for 75 Cents!

Mrs. Phillips being desirous, on account of the state of her health, to close out the sale of her volume of poems, "Under the Pines," has decided to reduce the price of the book during the holiday season to 75 cents, or half the original price. Doubtless many friends of the author, and all others desirous of possessing a copy of the only book of poems ever published in the northern part of Wisconsin, will avail themselves of this opportunity of procuring it at a price far below the cost of publication. The book is beautifully bound and printed. . . . ,

For sale at McCulloch's, McDonald's and Cadman's.

Stevens Point Daily Journal, 9 December 1876

"Under the Pines."

This is the title of a book of poems by Mrs. E. E. Phillips of Wisconsin, under the *nom de plume* of Ada J. Moore. We have been more than ordinarily interested in them, not only on account of the writer but also on account of the intrinsic merit of the poems themselves. Mrs. Phillips will be recognized by her pupils as a former preceptress of Brownington academy. She is the daughter of Rev. Dr. Hall of Brownington, and was brought up among our own green hills, of some of which she writes. She dedicates the book to her father in the following words: "To my loved and venerated father, Rev. Dr. Hall of Vermont, this little volume is affectionately dedicated, in the hope that it may brighten with a new pleasure the 80th year of a life of rare beauty and usefulness."

The book is made up of upwards of eighty short poems on as many different subjects, some drawn from nature, some from her early associations among the green hills of our own state; some are suggested by her new western home, and some by passing events. They are all full of the poetic element, and as pure as the falling snow-flakes. We know of no book more elevating in its tone, nor one with which those little snatches of time that every one has could be more profitably spent.

What picture can be pleasanter or more life-like that the following from a poem entitled, "Seed-time and Harvest:" . . . .

Here's another pretty picture, entitled "After the Rain:" . . . .

This little volume is full of gems. It is published by West & Co., of Milwaukee, printed and bound in fine style, with tinted paper and blue covers, and is altogether an ornament fit for the center table or as a gift to a friend. We presume arrangements will be made so that it can be sold in these parts.

Express and Standard [Newport, VT], 16 January 1877

Death of Mrs. Phillips.

The following tribute to the life and works of Mrs. Phillips is from the pen of Gen. A. G. Ellis, who had been acquainted with deceased during her entire residence in this city:

Our town was thrown into deep mourning on Friday morning, August 24th, by the announcement of the death of our dearly loved friend, Mrs. Phillips, wife of Dr. John Phillips; the event had been looked for truly, she having lingered in illness for many weeks; still when it came it thrilled us all with anguish, and yet we should not mourn as those without hope; for her life had been that of a true Christian; and while passing to the better land she could speak words of consolation and trust to her sorrowing friends.

But a few days since we had to indite the obituary of her honored father, Rev. Samuel Read Hall who had died at Brownington, Vermont, on the 24th of June. We joined mourning for him with deep respect for his elevated character and Christian virtues; but for her, our sorrows spring from long acquaintance; she came to reside among us in the freshness of early womanhood, with the bloom and graces of her youth and loveliness, challenging our admiration and esteem.

Ellen Eliza Hall, born at Andover, Massachusetts, Oct. 14, 1832, was married to Dr. John Phillips at Brownington, Vermont, Oct.4, 1854, and came here to reside that fall, and has been a constant and greatly beloved member of our society ever since—about 23 years. These lines but feebly portray her worth and excellence. The daughter of a distinguished educator, Rev. Samuel Read Hall, before mentioned, her education was carefully secured, and her mind cultivated in no ordinary degree:—not rudiments alone, but the more solid attainments of physics and philosophy adorned and strengthened her understanding. Yet her reticence and modest deportment was ever such, that nothing like display of pedantry appeared in her intercourse with society:—and her learning, if appearing at all, was only as an adornment of her eminent christian graces. It was only her more intimate friends and family that knew of her attainments in the exact sciences and the languages:—her beautiful poems, "Under the Pines," though only a fraction of her writing, are before the public—published, as we know, with much reluctance, and after repeated solicitations of her friends;—and written as they were only to beguile leisure hours, may nevertheless challenge criticism and do equal honor to her mind and heart.

To recite her works of charity, her labors of love, would only be to give a history of most of the benevolent enterprises among our lady friends, that have been had in our city over the last 20 years. Among those of a literary caste, it may not be inappropriate to cite that of our now excellent Library Association as an institution, to be credited, not wholly, but very largely to her efforts.

It would be almost superfluous to speak of her christian character to the people of Stevens Point.—the editor of the JOURNAL, in his brief notice of her death, has well said, "her list of friends was limited only by the number of her acquaintances:"—that "in her death a husband has lost a devoted wife, three children a loving mother, the poor a generous friend, and society a noble, christian woman." The Rev. Mr. Patch who preached her funeral sermon, who had known her long and well, also bore unqualified testimony to her worth.

The patience and even cheerfulness with which she endured a lingering illness testified her unwavering faith and trust in her Divine Lord, giving assurance to her surviving friends that while sensible of passing away from us, to join her loved ones gone before, she looked calmly to a *brighter world*, where there shall be neither sighing nor shadows—as she says in her own sweet song:

> "Heaven is free from shadows,
> All is perfect, pure ethereal *light:*—
> In the holy city shall every ransomed spirit
> Wear its blood bought robe, of spotless white,
> Where no falsehood staineth,
> Where the Saviour reigneth,
> Shadows shall not dwell."

Stevens Point Journal, 1 September 1877

DIED.

—"ADA J. MOORE."—The sad tidings come to us that Ellen E., wife of Dr. J. Phillips of Stevens' Point, Wis., and daughter of the late Rev. S. R. Hall of Brownington, died Aug. 20, 1877. Although not a native of Vermont, Mrs. Phillips spent most of her childhood and youth in Orleans county. Dr. Hall removed from Concord, N.H., to Craftsbury, Vt., and became pastor of the Congregational church at that place, when the subject of this sketch was six or seven years of age. Of an ardent, impulsive temperament, and remarkably strong in her affections, she was dearly loved by all who knew her. As a scholar, she was almost precocious, early showing rare talent in the acquirement of languages and in the composition both of prose and poetry. Many of the former students of Craftsbury academy remember with pleasure the slight figure, the prominent forehead, the twinkling black eyes, and the ready wit of Ellen Hall. Love of nature was with her almost a passion, and she revelled in the grand mountain scenery of her early home. Later in life, when she revisited these scenes, she said of Mount Mansfield:

> Silent and awed I sit, beneath the spell
> Of his vast presence, as a pilgrim bows
> Before the shrine to which his weary feet
> Have made their wonted pilgrimage.

When she was about twenty years of age she married Dr. Phillips, and went to her western home. Loving her husband almost to idolatry and receiving equal love in return, her cup of happiness might have been too full, but death took one after another of their children. Of a family of eleven sons and daughters but three survive her, the eldest, "Baby Florence" of her poems. From time to time after her marriage, contributions from her pen appeared in western papers under the *nom de plume* of Ada J. Moore. About two years ago she published her little book, "Under the Pines," of which Orleans county has a right to be proud, as many of those poems were written when she was a school girl at Craftsbury and Brownington. An appreciative notice of this book has already appeared in the EXPRESS & STANDARD. It is to be hoped that her many friends in this vicinity will have an opportunity to purchase this production of one, who in all but birth was a true daughter of Vermont. The poem which accompanies this was written on the fly leaf of a book belonging to a schoolmate, and never before published. It was written at Craftsbury in Nov. 1852:

DEAR SISTER.
WRITTEN ON THE FLY LEAF OF A BOOK
BELONGING TO A SCHOOLMATE

Dear Sister. Mid the laughing hours
That wing their flight so swiftly by,
Strewing the student's path with flowers,
And kindling joy in many an eye;
There cometh one with saddened mien,
With tearful eye and heavy heart,
Tinging with sadness all the scene—
It is the hour when we must part.

Must part! What magic in a word
To pale the cheek and dim the eye,
To bid the spirit's depths be stirred
And every thought of pleasure fly!
Oh, there is untold mystery
In many a sight and sound of life,
But strangest, saddest, still must be
Affection's tearful parting strife.

Awhile, amid earth's ceaseless change,
Two of a scattered band we've met,
Have sought the fields of thought to range,
And tasted of joys we'll ne'er forget.
We part, but will not say *farewell,*
For in the realms of thought and love
Our spirits still shall mingling dwell,
And hope to meet for aye above.

Craftsbury, Vermont, November 1852
Express and Standard, 2 October 1877

Acknowledgments

The editors would like to thank the Portage County Historical Society, without whose book sale we never would have come across the first edition of *Under the Pines* and whose continued work in local history keeps Portage County's stories alive. Many thanks to the Nelis R. Kampenga University Archives and Area Research Center at the University of Wisconsin–Stevens Point for helping us access original and microfilm copies of Stevens Point area newspapers as well as archival documents related to the Phillips family. Much appreciation also to The Wisconsin Historical Society for providing microfilm reels of other Wisconsin newspapers. And thank you to Dr. Ross Tangedal and the excellent editorial team at Cornerstone Press led by Karlie Harpold.

About the Editors

M. WADE MAHON is Professor of English at the University of Wisconsin–Stevens Point. He teaches rhetorical theory, composition, eighteenth-century British and Irish literature, and legal writing. In 2024, he published *Informal Education in Eighteenth-Century Ireland* with Palgrave Macmillan. Also in 2024 he published an article in *Eighteenth Century Ireland* on eighteenth-century Irish poet Thomas Spring, who, like Ellen Phillips, deserves greater recognition.

LILLIAN S. MAHON is a senior at the University of Wisconsin–Stevens Point. She is majoring in environmental education and interpretation, with a history and museum studies minor. She is active in the Portage County Historical Society. In 2024 and 2025 she played viola in the UWSP Orchestra. The jug band with whom she performs won a national competition in 2025.